I0138635

THE HACK OF HUMANITY

Unveiling the Plot Against
The Human Race

THE HACK OF HUMANITY

*UNVEILING THE PLOT AGAINST
THE HUMAN RACE*

Ruthven J. Roy

REHOBOTH
PUBLISHING

The Hack of Humanity: *Unveiling the Plot Against the Human Race*
Copyright © 2020 by Ruthven J. Roy

ISBN   Hardcover   978-0-9888132-7-4
                                     0-9888132-7-0

Rehoboth Publishing, LLC
P.O. Box 33
Berrien Springs, MI 49103

For additional copies of this book or for author speaking engagements write to: royjrbooks@gmail.com, or visit www.roybooks.com

CONTENTS

Introduction vii

Chapter One
The Hacking Framework 11

Chapter Two
God's Creative Purpose for Humanity 17

Chapter Three
God's Order of Operation in Creation 29

Chapter Four
God's Order of Operation in Humanity 39

Chapter Five
Enter the Master Hacker 51

Chapter Six
How Satan Hacked Humanity 63

Chapter Seven
Understanding the Virus in Humanity 83

Chapter Eight
Satan's Viral Support System 111

Chapter Nine
The Hack and Identity Corruption 133

Chapter Ten
The Hack and Human Restlessness 153

Chapter Eleven
The Only Way Out 171

In Dedication

To

My Forever Friend, my advantageous Helper,
Teacher and faithful Guide to ALL Truth,
The Holy Spirit

All Humanity—Hacked and unaware of it

Acknowledgments

Every book I have ever written was made possible only through the wisdom, revelation and guidance of my forever Teacher and Friend. This one is no exception. Thank You Holy Spirit for Your prevailing influence over my inner life in Christ Jesus, the only truth of my existence.

Special thanks to my inner circle—Lyris, Lyrisa, Mirisa, Charisa, Fabiaye, Renee and Aaron—for your inspiration, candid support and feedback, and for adding value and meaning to all I do. You are my other reason for staying focused and faithful to the only Life that gives meaning to all others—JESUS.

To my Network Discipling Ministries family: How could I have completed this book without you being the spiritual sounding board, validation and living illustration of every revelation that I share through this work. Thank you for all you continue to show and teach me.

The material production of this manuscript was not possible without the faithful work of my editorial team who helped me to process and refine its many concepts. A special shout out the point man and designer of every book I have written, Emmerson Cyrille. You are the best in my book. Thanks to all of you.

Introduction

Have you ever tried desperately to fall asleep but just simply couldn't? It was frustrating to say the least, wasn't it? *"Why can't I shut off my own mind when I really want to fall asleep?"* What about the ongoing struggle to commit to resolutions and to succeed in achieving set goals but failing miserably to do so? We have all been there, haven't we? How about trying to maintain a positive outlook over a particular situation only to be overcome by doubt, fear, guilt and even depression? All of these scenarios beg for the answer to this all-important question: How much control do we really have over our own lives or the bodies that we live in?

Regardless of race, religious belief or unbelief, or socio-economic status, our daily experiences show that we share the common fate of humanity—victims of oppressive, unwelcome enslavement and ongoing devious, negative thoughts and behaviors. Quite often we find ourselves going down the proverbial "rabbit hole" to end up in situations that we know we have no business being in but find ourselves there anyway. Someone said to me very recently, "Sir, how come I always seem to attract fake people into my life?" My response, though genuine, may have come as a surprise to my inquirer. I responded, "have you ever considered the possibility that perhaps some element of falsehood also exists in you?" After a moment of reflection, and with great humility, the individual was able to identify how this unperceived oversight may have played a significant role in her personal interactions with others.

Our issue of concern may not be negative or evil attractions but perhaps addictive or uncontrollable behavior. That issue may even manifest itself as some other repulsive element in our life that just seems impossible for us to shake. The way forward often appears quite obscure and probably terrifying due to the fear that this "demon" may show up in the wrong place and at the wrong time, to embarrass or even hurt us. This is a very real issue for everyday people that leaves an unsettling fear over the future.

However, it is rather interesting to see how the Bible sheds light on this very thing. In his Gospel, John's testimony of Jesus Christ seems to confirm this troubling human outlook, that there is something mysteriously evil and destructive lurking within humanity. It is an element so dastardly repulsive that even the Savior recoils from it. He wrote:

> *23Now when He was in Jerusalem at the Passover, during the feast, many believed in His name when they saw the signs which He did. 24But Jesus did not commit Himself to them, because* **He knew all men [humanity],** *25and had no need that anyone should testify of man [humanity], for* **He knew what was in man [humanity].**

John 2:23-25.

What is it that Christ identified in humanity that gave Him such dim perspective of the human race? The purpose of this book is to explore what this inherent, objectionable element really is. It will also reveal a clear, comprehensive, behind-the-scene look at the demonic activities working against our noblest thoughts and intentions, prompting our most sinful, insidious behaviors. However, in order to facilitate an easy understanding of this book, I have chosen to use the language of computer technology to paint very vivid pictures of Satan's engagement, infiltration and manipulation of our lives. This is what gave rise to the title of the book, **The Hack[1] of Humanity.**

Contextually, this book will expose Satan's plot against the human race. It will show how the evil one gained unauthorized access (hacked) into the soul of humanity, and set about to control, steal, kill and destroy the masterpiece of God's creation—Adam and his descendants. Through lies and artful deception the devil planted in the human psyche a deadly virus, which he triggers continuously to control the thinking and behaviors of his subjects.

God has given us the only way out of the devil's uncompromising, oppressive servitude, and He desires that every reader experience the delightful liberty He provides through His free Gift for humanity's salvation. It is my joyous privilege to share this wonderful freedom with you. I invite you to join me on this journey through the pages of this book.

---

[1]The term "hack" means *to gain unauthorized access to or control over computer network security systems for some illicit or malicious purpose—to steal, destroy or even prevent authorized users from accessing the system.*

"The thief does not come except to steal, and to kill, and to destroy. I have come that they may have life, and that they may have it more abundantly"

John 10:10

1

The Hacking Framework

Our current technological and computer age has made our world a very small global village that facilitates enhanced human connections. It also places information and knowledge at the fingertips of anyone seeking enlightenment on any particular subject. Every major system of operation that keeps our world centers busy making life on this planet possible is currently digitized for optimum capacity, efficiency and productivity.

Global political systems, communication systems, travel systems, governing systems, financial systems, commercial systems, food systems, water systems, environmental systems, health systems—just to name a few—depend heavily, if not completely, on electronic technology and the efficient transmission of information among all the global systems. Information travels at lightning speed all over the world to the convenience of all who avail themselves of the gadgets and instruments of its superhighway. Moreover, the competitive pressure among nations for global dominance is so overwhelmingly strong that there is absolutely no way for them to go back to outdated technology for information gathering and transmission. The electronic and computer age is here to stay, and the one who rules cyber space has the global edge.

However, in spite of its commanding and enduring successes and future optimism, our current technological age faces very real dangers that threaten its smooth functionality in operating the world systems so necessary for human survival. On a personal level, everyone is happy about the conveniences that their collection of electronic devices provides for day-to-day living, until the devices fail or the infrastructure that supports them is suddenly disrupted.

Because of the heavy global dependence on the electronic activities taking place in cyber space, and the potential for so many things to go wrong at very rapid pace, communities and people are becoming increasingly guarded in the use of their electronic devices. There is also growing distrust towards the managers of the computerized global systems in their ability to faithfully discharge their duty in safeguarding the personal and private information of their patrons.

Enter the Hackers

In recent times our world has seen a dramatic rise in cyber hacking. This phenomenon places increasing pressure on world governments, social and business leaders and entities to protect themselves from the fallout of the deadly, unwarranted attacks of hackers. During the 2016 Presidential campaign in the United States of America, cyber hacking got major domestic and international attention when Russian operatives hacked into the Democratic National Committee (DNC) computer network, stole and released information to compromise Hillary Clinton's Presidential bid. Moreover, hackers also infiltrated social media, Facebook in particular, and disseminated fake information to sway voters to vote for a particular candidate.

Virtual hacking has become a very real threat to all global computerized systems. Cyber warfare is now an existential threat to the major nations of our world. In 2019 the city council of Riviera Beach, Florida, USA paid hackers $600,000 in order to regain control of its captured computer network. The city of Baltimore spent a whopping $18 million in network repairs after hackers breeched their system and extorted $100,000 in ransom money.

Recently, my wife's computer was hacked, and we were locked out completely from the machine. The hacker was posting pornographic images on the screen, and whenever we tried to erase them, they were replaced by many, many more. I tried shutting the computer down, but the hacker would only turn it on again. Finally, the perpetrator sent a message to us which demanded payment of a tidy sum before control of the computer could be returned to us. This last scenario surely taught me some precious lessons which I will share throughout this book. Once your PC or computer network is hacked, it is forever compromised, and you will never have complete control over it again without the consent of the hacker. Needless to say, we had to purchase a brand-new PC for my wife and change her username and password for every one of her online accounts. Such is the lot of many who have experienced this problem.

The Ultimate Hacker

"The 'thief' does not come except to steal, and to kill, and to destroy..."

John 10:10

In the above scripture, Jesus paints a perfect picture of the character of the evil one that forms the operating philosophy of modern-day hackers. Satan is not only a thief of every good gift of God for the human family, but he is also a remorseless oppressor and murderer of the same. Through his masterful deception, he has made humanity a hacked job, the very habitation of a hacked system of operation that produces all types of evil, destruction, pain and death in the earth. Here is how the Bible describes mankind after Satan's hacking of the human soul:

> *Then the Lord saw that the wickedness of man was great in the earth, and that <u>every intent</u> of the thoughts of his heart was only <u>evil continually</u>.*

> Genesis 6:5

> *The heart is <u>deceitful</u> above all things, and <u>desperately wicked</u>;* **Who can know it?**

> Jeremiah 17:9

The hack of humanity is a very real phenomenon, even more real than the electronic hacking of global computerized systems. It is because of the depravity produced by the human hack that all other forms of hacking are even possible. When we contemplate the grave danger and untold damage caused by individual hackers all over the world, we can only imagine what

Through his masterful deception, he has made humanity a hacked job, the very habitation of a hacked system of operation that produces all types of evil, destruction, pain and death in the earth.

the potential for wanton destruction is when we consider that all humanity has been hacked by the evil one.

In spite of all the human advancements and achievements that often boggle the mind, our modern world has become a huge gathering place of human pain, suffering and tragedy. The staggering rise of intense hatred, barefaced moral degradation, and inhumane behaviors are very dark reflections of the sinister forces at work within the human soul. These unseen powers are driving people to all types of deadly excesses that pose serious threat to our very existence on this planet.

The very sad and uncomfortable truth is that humanity is the victim of demonic hacking, and the masses are totally unaware of it. The devious enemy of our souls will not allow us the luxury of knowing that we are being manipulated and controlled by forces we cannot discern by mere human perception or intelligence. In addition, he deceives many into believing that they are the singular masters of their own destinies. Unknowingly, humanity is totally deluded, victimized and oppressed and willingly cooperates with its oppressor in its degradation and demise.

How and why we got here is the compelling storyline of this book. We will also be introduced to the initial steps we can take to resist and neutralize the hacking schemes of the evil one.

Then God said, *"Let Us make man in Our image, according to Our likeness; let them have dominion over the fish of the sea, over the birds of the air, and over the cattle, over all the earth and over every creeping thing that creeps on the earth."*

Genesis 1:26

2

God's Creative Purpose for Humanity

The Bible declares, without apology or equivocation, that *"in the beginning God created the heavens and the earth"* (Genesis 1:1). In this one cogent statement it accounts for the existence of our world and the authoritative power of the supreme, infallible Creator who called it into being— God.

> *For this is what the Lord says—He who created the heavens, He is God; He who fashioned and made the earth, He founded it; He did not create it to be empty, but formed it to be inhabited—He says: "I am the Lord, and there is no other".*

Isaiah 45:18, NIV

In the above scripture, the prophet Isaiah explains four fundamental truths about the Creator of heaven and earth: (1) The Creator of heaven and earth is God; (2) He designed and established the earth. (3) He created the earth to be inhabited; and (4) There is absolutely no other God beside Him. He is sovereign and supreme and is not silent about it. *"...Is there a God besides Me? Indeed, there is no other Rock; I know not one (Isaiah 44:8). "It was I who made the earth and created the people upon it; It was my hands that stretched out the heavens; I gave the order to all their host"* (Isaiah 45:12, NASB, Revised Edition).

Clearly, the God who created, designed and established our world is not apologetic about who He is and what He does. Moreover, He is intently purposeful in all His actions. He does absolutely nothing off of a whim or as an after-thought. As a matter of fact, the Bible describes Him as the God who knows the end of a thing from the very beginning of that thing. God

the God who created, designed and establish our world is not apologetic about who He is and what He does.

always begins a thing from the standpoint of the end that the thing serves. He NEVER begins and then "wonders" how it would end; but He Who transcends space and time first designs the end of a thing and then works with that end in view.

> *"Remember this, and show yourselves men; Recall to mind, O you transgressors. ⁹Remember the former things of old, For I am God, and there is no other; I am God, and there is none like Me, ¹⁰**Declaring the end from the beginning, And from ancient times things that are not yet done,** Saying, 'My counsel [purpose] shall stand, And I will do all My pleasure,' ¹¹Calling a bird of prey from the east, The man who executes My counsel [purpose], from a far country. Indeed, I have spoken it; I will also bring it to pass. I have purposed it; I will also do it."*

> Isaiah 46:8-11, NKJV, emphasis mine

The above scripture shines the spotlight on God's supremacy, absolute authority and immaculate purposefulness. It reveals that God's purposes are grounded in His perfect knowledge of everything and everyone, declaring *"from ancient times things that are not yet done."* His omnipresence and omniscience defy human logic, and His foreknowledge and precise operations often frustrate human understanding. Albeit, in His sovereign authority He operates totally independent of human inputs, objections or criticisms. *"Indeed, I have spoken it; I will also bring it to pass. I have purposed it; I will also do it"* (Isaiah

> *God always begin a thing from the standpoint of the end that the thing serves.*

46:11). It is this transcendent, omnipotent, omnipresent, omniscience God Who, in the beginning of time, created the heavens and the earth. Isaiah said, *He did not create it to be empty, but formed it to be inhabited* (Isaiah 45:18).

In His Image and Likeness

Then God said, *"Let Us make man in Our image, according to Our likeness..."*

Genesis 1:26

In keeping with His divine purpose, God created a world of flawless beauty for the inhabitants He had in mind to inherit and enjoy it. The Bible says when *God saw all that he had made... behold, it was very good* (Genesis 1:31). However, the primary objective of God's creation was not the beautiful world that He had made, but the ultimate reason for which he made it—humankind.

It is very interesting to note that God did not create

the first man, Adam, and then decide to design a world to accommodate his needs; but He created the world and everything in it with Adam in view. Everything necessary for Adam's sustenance, enjoyment, mental and physical engagements was present before he appeared on the earth. At the appropriate time God made the most profound declaration: *"Let Us make man in Our image, according to Our likeness..."* (Genesis 1:26). At a glance this may seem as a very simple statement; but that is infinitely far from the case. Hidden in this very inconspicuous proclamation is the seed of God's awe-inspiring purpose for humanity. So, let us examine this sentence more closely.

in His sovereign authority God operates totally independent of human inputs, objections or criticisms.

Let Us:

First of all, the statement is a declaration that conveys plurality of intention—*Let Us make man in Our image, according to Our likeness*. This plurality communicates the inherent multiplicity of God's Spirit nature, expressing itself three-dimensionally in the Divine personalities of Father, Son and Holy Spirit. Moreover, God, the Divine Spirit, is also the wellspring of every living being in heaven and on earth. The Apostle Paul says that in God, *every family in heaven and earth derives its name [existence]* (Ephesians 3:15, brackets mine). The Hebrew word for God in Genesis 1:26 is *Elohim*, the plural of *Eloah*,

God did not create the first man, Adam, and then decided to design a world to accommodate his needs; but He created the world and everything in it with Adam in view.

and is consistent with that usage throughout the Old Testament. Although God, in the Hebrew mind is One, He is always expressed as a plurality, which points to His inherent multi-productive, life-giving Spirit nature.

Consequently, when God *(Elohim)* said, *"Let Us make man in Our image, according to Our likeness,"* the declaration had the unifying force of the Divine personalities of Father, Son and Holy Spirit behind it. These were the life-giving words of the eternal, omnipotent God *(Elohim)* activating the launch of human history upon the newly created earth.

Image and Likeness:

The Bible clearly states that God is a Spirit (John 4:24). Therefore, nothing material could be used in any way to adequately represent Him. To suggest or attempt such representation would be nothing short of a gross human error. In his parting words to the children of Israel, Moses gave them stern warning with regard to making such a drastic blunder.

> *[15]Take careful heed to yourselves, for you saw no form when the Lord spoke to you at Horeb out of the midst of the fire, [16]lest you act corruptly and make for yourselves a **carved image** in the **form of any figure:** the likeness of male or female, [17]the likeness of any animal that is on the earth or the likeness of any winged bird that flies in the air, [18]the likeness of anything that creeps on the ground or the likeness of any fish that is in the water beneath the earth. [19]And take heed,*

lest you lift your eyes to heaven, and when you see <u>the sun</u>, the <u>moon</u>, and <u>the stars, all the host of heaven</u>, you feel driven to worship them and serve them, which the Lord your God has given to all the peoples under the whole heaven as a heritage.

Deuteronomy 4:15-19, emphasis mine

Moses gave Israel quite a comprehensive negative list of material objects from which one could be tempted to make any physical representation of God. Lest they missed anything in the list, God was very careful to mention that no form of any figure or the likeness of male or female should be made as an image of the Great "I AM." From this informative account, it seems quite plausible to deduce that the phrase "image and likeness" in Genesis 1:26 must be taken to represent characteristics of God other than physical features and appearance.

Simply put, image refers to the righteous, Spirit nature or character of God, and likeness to the way God's nature in humanity expresses itself. I will deal with these two very important elements of humanity in greater detail in the next chapter.

Image = God's righteous Spirit nature
Likeness = Outward expression of God's Spirit nature in humanity

God's Creative Purpose

*"...let them **have dominion** over the fish of the sea, over the birds of the air, and over the cattle,*

*over all the earth and over every creeping thing
that creeps on the earth."*

Genesis 1:26

Why did God create man in His own image and
according to His likeness? Primarily, it was God's simple, yet
very profound, purpose to express the
reality of His own life through humanity—
to express godliness or godlikeness on
earth as it is expressed in heaven. As
such, God's image was the foundation
of Adam's identity and personhood,
and his unerring source of knowledge,
wisdom and direction. Additionally, God
also shared His image with humanity to
establish His place of connection and communion with His
earthly family. Consequently, He endowed Adam with His
own nature so that he and his generations would be the
extension of God's sovereign rule over all creation. What an
unimaginable lofty ideal for humanity! What magnanimous
love! *"...let them have dominion..."* is a declaration of supreme
government over the earth and every living thing on it.

> *He endowed
> Adam with His
> own nature so
> that he and his
> generations would
> be the extension
> of God's sovereign
> rule over all
> creation.*

> [27]*So God created man in His <u>own image</u>; in <u>the
> image of God</u> He created him; male and female
> He created them.* [28]*Then God blessed them, and
> God said to them, "Be fruitful and multiply;* **fill
> the earth** *and* **subdue it***;* **have dominion** *over the
> fish of the sea, over the birds of the air, and* **over
> every living thing that moves on the earth."**

Genesis 1:27, 28, emphasis mine

In Genesis 1:26, God made a declaration concerning not only the nature and characteristic of humanity that were akin to His, but also the lofty purpose for which He assigned both to the race. In that announcement, He spoke about humanity ruling over all creation. However, there is a significant difference in how the announcement is repeated in Genesis 1:28. Here, God is not simply making a statement; He is giving a direct command: *"...fill the earth... subdue it... have dominion... over every living thing that moves on the earth."*

Humanity's creative purpose was to fill and dominate the earth as God fills and dominates the vast universe.

God extended Himself and His authority through Adam and his generations, giving them full stewardship of all creation. Humanity's creative purpose was to fill and dominate the earth as God fills and dominates the vast universe. The source of Adam's knowledge, wisdom, power and authority was grounded in the perfect union of his spirit with the Spirit of his maker.

Adam's Vocal Authority:

Like his Creator, Adam was an authoritative speaking spirit, yet unlike Him, Adam had a body-house. Just as God created and upholds the world by the word of His power, so Adam was to exercise his dominion over the earth and every living thing by the word of his mouth. In keeping with this unique relationship and the execution of his purpose in the earth, God gave Adam the opportunity to exercise his vocal authority.

[19]Out of the ground the Lord God formed every

*beast of the field and every bird of the air and brought them to Adam to see what he would call them. And **whatever** Adam <u>called each living creature, that was its name</u>.*

Genesis 2:19, emphasis mine

It is very vital to establish two very important things about this divine encounter. (1) Adam did not have to figure out what names he needed to assign to the birds and animals that God paraded before him. His perfect spirit union with the Fountain of all knowledge and wisdom availed him with the capacity and ability to name every one of earth's living creatures. (2) Adam's words had

Like his Creator, Adam was an authoritative, speaking spirit, yet unlike Him, Adam had a body-house.

immediate effects on the creatures, confirming not only their names, but also the unique characteristics associated with the names. In other words, the naming of the dog was aligned perfectly with the distinctive features of the dog, and not those of a cat; and the same was true for the naming of all the other creatures.

In the larger scheme of things, Adam and his descendants were assigned the awesome task of filling,

It was God's eternal purpose for mankind to experience a quality of life that was akin to His right here on earth.

subduing and ruling over the earth and its living creatures. Their ability to speak as the expression of their Father was the avenue by which they were to execute their godlike function. It was God's eternal purpose for mankind to experience a quality of life that was akin to His right here on earth. However, something went terribly wrong. A demonic mastermind devised a crafty plot against the race, to steal, undermine and destroy the lofty purpose God envisioned for humanity. The rest of this book will unmask this subversive scheme and reveal God's perfect, complete solution for this "Hack of Humanity".

Hast thou not known? hast thou not heard, that the everlasting God, the LORD, the Creator of the ends of the earth, fainteth not, neither is weary? There is no searching of his understanding.

Isaiah 40:28, KJV

3

God's Order of Operation in Creation

We have already seen from the previous chapter that the God of our creation is the God of purpose, *with Whom is no variation or shadow of turning* (James 1:17). In this chapter, we will turn our attention to the orderly unfolding of His purposes which are sure and steadfast. Through His prophet Isaiah, God said: ...'*My purpose will be established, and I will accomplish all My good pleasure'; ¹¹Calling a bird of prey from the east, The man of My purpose from a far country. Truly I have spoken; truly I will bring it to pass. I have planned it, surely I will do it* (Isaiah 46:10, 11, NASB, emphasis mine).

Truly, all God's works are done with immaculate precision and in divine perfection. They operate in seamless harmony with His eternal will and purpose. Additionally, all God's purposes are driven by His absolute knowledge and limitless understanding of everything. The Psalmist David plainly stated, *"such knowledge is too wonderful for me; It is high, I cannot attain it"* (SEE Psalm 139:1-6). The apostle Paul says that *ALL the treasures of wisdom and knowledge* are hidden in Him (Colossians 2:3). Really, no human mind is capable of

> all God's works are done with immaculate precision and in divine perfection. They operate in seamless harmony with His eternal will and purpose.

comprehending the unfathomable depth and vastness of God's wisdom, knowledge and understanding. Moreover, the prophet Isaiah says that *"...there is no searching of His understanding"* (Isaiah 40:28).

In light of this realization, there is categorically no distortion, confusion or misalignment of anything God does, and nowhere is this more clearly seen than in His ordered creation of our world and of humanity. As we examine the Genesis account of God's magnificent handiworks, we can clearly see the order and exactness of all His operations.

God's Order in the Heavens and on the Earth

It is very important to note that our world is a "word" creation. God spoke into existence the earth, the sea and the sky and everything they contained. Absolutely nothing of the original creation existed apart from His spoken word. The Bible clearly testifies to this fact:

> *[6]By the word of the Lord the heavens were made, And all the host of them by the breath of His mouth. [7]He gathers the waters of the sea together as a heap; He lays up the deep in storehouses. [8]Let all the earth fear the Lord; Let all the inhabitants of the world stand in awe of Him. [9]For He spoke, and it was done; He commanded, and it stood fast.*
>
> Psalm 33:6-9, emphasis mine

> *[3]By faith we understand that the worlds were framed by the word of God, so that the things*

which are seen were not made of things which are visible.

Hebrews 11:3, emphasis mine

Clearly, God's words are profoundly powerful. They are *spirit and life* (John 6:63)—that is, life-producing and life-affecting. According to the above scripture from Hebrews, God not only form the ages of all existence by the word of His mouth, but He also formed them from absolutely nothing. In other words, God is capable of creating something from nothing, and turning to nothing something that already exists—all by speaking. In Genesis 1, nine times it is recorded that God spoke (*God said*), and at the end of His speaking, the Bible records that what He said became or appeared. (SEE Genesis 1:3, 6, 9, 11, 14, 20, 24, 26, 29). Let us examine God's order, paying attention to the word "*Then*" before each of His declarations. "*Then*" is indicative of a natural progression in the order of things:

> God's words are profoundly powerful. They are spirit and life (John 6:63)—that is, life-producing and life-affecting.

1. Genesis 1:3 - *Then God said, "Let there be light..."* Light appeared first because without light there could be absolutely no life. It is also very important to note that this light was not that produced by the sun (which was created on the 4th day) but typified the very presence of God—who is Light (1 John 1:5)— confronting and impacting the chaotic darkness at the beginning of time.

2. Genesis 1:6 - *Then God said, "Let there be a firmament..."* The firmament represented the

atmospheric heavens that separated the waters above it from the waters beneath it.

3. Genesis 1:9 – *Then God said, "Let the waters under the heavens be gathered together into one place, and let the dry land appear..."* The dry land and the sea were next in order as God created the perfect environment to sustain all life forms He purposed to call into existence. He also set firm the boundaries of the sea so that its waters would not engulf the land.

4. Genesis 1:11 – *Then God said, "Let the earth bring forth grass, the herb that yields seed, and the fruit tree that yields fruit according to its kind, whose seed is in itself, on the earth"...*Lush vegetation, fruit trees with fruits containing seeds dressed the bare earth with beauty and food.

5. Genesis 1:14, 15 – *Then God said, "Let there be lights in the firmament of the heavens to divide the day from the night; and let them be for signs and seasons, and for days and years; ¹⁵and let them be for lights in the firmament of the heavens to give light on the earth"* – The sun, moon and stars were next in line to govern the day and night, signs, seasons, months and years. The word of God still stands firm in this regard for the signs and the seasons are still with us, and meteorologists and astrologists still rely on them for their forecasting.

6. Genesis 1:20 – *Then God said, "Let the waters abound with an abundance of living creatures, and let birds fly above the earth across the face of the firmament of the heavens."* – In orderly progression God established the habitation for the air and sea

creatures before calling them into existence.

7. <u>Genesis 1:24</u> – *Then God said, "Let the earth bring forth the living creature according to its kind: cattle and creeping thing and beast of the earth, each according to its kind..."* – As with the air and the sea, so also with the earth. God provided the living environment for creatures great and small before declaring their presence on the earth.

8. <u>Genesis 1:26</u> – *Then God said, "Let Us make man in Our image, according to Our likeness..."* – God reserved for last what was the crowning act of His creation—humankind. Everything that God created before the arrival of Adam was made for his use, recreation and enjoyment. As was previously stated in chapter 2, God's end always determines His beginning. Purpose always precedes production. Everything God did during creation was for the singular purpose of serving the man He created in His own image and after His likeness. What a lofty God-view of humanity! Ponder the awesomeness and value of our creation and your presence in the world!

Why Is "Order of Operation" So Important and Necessary?

The answer to this critical question will prove quite invaluable to the way we deal with current issues and situations in our lives. Most people tackle their life's problems purely by logical reasoning and this approach often leads to mental confusion, stress and other emotional and physical ailments. Whenever we cannot figure something out through human reason it produces stressful thoughts which impact

God's end always determines His beginning. Purpose always precedes production. Everything God did during creation was for the singular purpose of serving the man He created in His own image and after His likeness.

our brain and interfere with the orderly functions of our body. Many are ignorant of the fact that they are unconsciously programmed to deal with life in this very unnatural and unhealthy way. As a former mathematics teacher for many, many years I also saw that most of my students brought the same approach to the classroom in their attempt to solve basic mathematical operations. Here is a typical example to illustrate this point. I have tried it in many of my seminars and it proves true every time. I also ask you my readers to try to solve the problem below without the use of a calculator or cell phone:

Solve 18 – 2 x 3 + 6 ÷ 3

Logically, most people will solve the problem by following the mathematical operation in the order of the sign following each number. Consequently, they will first subtract 2 from 18 and get **16**; then multiply 16 by 3 and get **48.** They will then add 6 to 48 and get **54**, and then they will divide 54 by 3 and get **18** as their final answer. What answer did you get? If you also got **18**, then that answer is not mathematically correct. Why? Because your logical approach did not follow the basic mathematical rule for numbers manipulation called "order of operations."

This rule requires doing the operation of numbers in Parenthesis, if present, first; then numbers with Exponents, if present; followed by numbers with Multiplication or Division in their order; and lastly, numbers with Addition or

Subtraction in their order. The first letter of each of these operations forms the acronym PEMDAS, or the memory line, **P**lease **E**xcuse **M**y **D**ear **A**unt **S**ally. Others may choose to use another acronym, BOMDAS, which amounts to the same result— viz, Brackets (another name for Parenthesis), Orders (another name

Whenever we cannot figure out something through human reason it produces stressful thoughts which impacts our brain and interferes with the orderly functions of our body.

for Exponents), Multiplication, Division, Addition and Subtraction. Additionally, the order of Multiplication and Division are reversible; the same holds true for the order of Addition and Subtraction.

When we apply the "order of operation" rule to the above problem, the result is quite different from 18. Since there are no parenthesis or exponents we do not have to worry about those operations. All we have is multiplication and division, and addition and subtraction. Consequently, we must multiply 2 by 3 first and get **6**; then we divide 6 by 3 and get **2**. Now we end up with 18 – **6 + 2**. When we subtract 6 from 18 and we get **12**, and we add 12 to 2 we get **14** as our final answer, very different from **18**.

Therefore, 18 – 2 x 3 + 6 ÷ 3 = **14**, and NOT **18**

The lesson here is very clear. In mathematics, if one fails to follow the "order of operation" his attempt at solving any problem will ALWAYS fall short of the correct solution. His answers will be wrong every time. Failure to know and follow the "order of operation" in math has brought frustration and discouragement to countless students of the subject, many of whom have become and remain very math averse.

The Real Point:

Just as there is an "order of operation" in mathematics and other fields of study, God also has an "order of operation" in the heavens, on the earth, and also in humankind whom He ordained to rule over all creation. What is true in mathematical science regarding "order of operation" also holds true in God's ordered creation. If one fails to follow God's "order of operation" in creation and in humanity, his attempts at solving life's problems will ALWAYS fall short of finding life's true joy and lasting fulfillment. The results could often be chaotic, disastrous, and even quite deadly. Because of Adam's sinful legacy to his descendants, all humanity lives in rebellion of God's "order of operation" in every one of the aforementioned spheres, and as a direct result we have all types of demonic and man-made disasters in our world.

> [19]*For all creation is waiting eagerly for that future day when God will reveal who his children really are.* [20]*Against its will, all creation was subjected to God's curse. But with eager hope,* [21]*the creation looks forward to the day when it will join God's children in glorious freedom from death and decay.* [22]*For we know that all creation has been groaning as in the pains of childbirth right up to the present time.*
>
> Romans 8:19-22, NLT[2], emphasis mine

---

[2]New Living Translation of the Holy Bible.

We do not have to look far to see and know that our world is in terrible shape. The constant threat of war and global annihilation, the frightening growth of climate catastrophes, the gross inhumanity of people against one another, the unabashed wantonness of immoral and criminal behavior, the insidious blurring of truth and the treasonous unthreading of the moral fibers that hold our societies together, are some of the current situations challenging the best governments of our world. All this is due to the sinister plot against humanity that has predisposed the race to live in rebellion against God and in total violation of His "order of operation" pertaining to His creation.

If one fails to follow God's "order of operation" in creation and in humanity his attempts at solving life's problems will ALWAYS fall short of finding life's true joy and lasting fulfillment.

And the Lord God formed man of the dust of the ground, and breathed into his nostrils the breath of life; and man became a living being.

Genesis 2:7

4

God's Order of Operation in Humanity

*And the Lord God formed man of the dust of the
ground, and breathed into his nostrils the breath
of life; and man became a living being.*

Genesis 2:7

In Genesis 1:26, we witness God making the
declarative statement regarding the existence and purpose
of humankind. Then God said, *"Let Us make man in Our
image, according to Our likeness; let them have dominion
over the fish of the sea, over the birds of the air, and over
the cattle, over all the earth and over every creeping thing
that creeps on the earth."* Let us now take a closer look at
the order by which man was created.

Habitation Precedes Presence:

It is quite noteworthy that just as God formed the
habitation of the earth before putting living creatures on
it, so He formed the habitation of man (his body) before
putting the reality of his presence in it. The main text for this
section states that *the Lord God formed man of the dust of*

THE HACK OF HUMANITY

the ground... (Genesis 2:7). This is a very clear reference to Adam's body-house and is very distinct from, yet uniquely connected to, what God did after He formed it.

Although all the organs (including the brain) of Adam's body were present and intact, they were completely lifeless because the spirit of who Adam really was did not yet occupy it. If I could use a rudimentary analogy, Adam's body was like a house filled with furniture and utensils but without the living presence of the owner. Everything in the house is useless until the owner occupies it. So it was with Adam. He could not be a complete whole until the presence of his spirit entered his body-house.

...just as God formed the habitation of the earth before putting living creatures on it, so He formed the habitation of man (his body) before putting the reality of his presence in it.

This simple analogy comes to life in the Apostle Paul's musings of the believer's guaranteed future life when his earthy body-house falls away in death.

> *¹For **we** know that when this <u>earthly tent</u> **we** <u>live in</u> is taken down (that is, when **we** die and leave this earthly body), **we** will have <u>a house</u> in heaven, an <u>eternal body</u> made for us by God himself and not by human hands. ²**We** grow weary in our present bodies, and **we** long to put on our heavenly bodies <u>like new clothing</u>. ³For **we** will <u>put on</u> heavenly bodies; **we** will not be **spirits** <u>without bodies</u>. ⁴While **we** <u>live in these earthly bodies</u>, **we** groan and sigh, but it's not that **we** want to*

*die and get rid of these <u>bodies that clothe us</u>. Rather, **we** want to put on our <u>new bodies</u> so that these <u>dying bodies</u> will be swallowed up by life. [5]God Himself has prepared us for this, and as a guarantee He has given us his Holy Spirit.*

2 Corinthians 5:1-5, NLT, emphasis mine

From the above scripture, it is very evident that there is a very clear distinction between the "we" who live in the "earthly tent" (clay body) and the tent itself. "We" who live in these bodies groan because of the challenges posed by their physical degradation. However, "we" do not want to roam the earth as naked spirits without body-houses, but "we" long to be "clothed" with our eternal body-houses from heaven. "We" need our present, deteriorating body-houses for the physical manifestation of the expressions of our Godlike spirits as "we" interact with our material world; but "we" long for something far better—bodies not subject to death or corruption.

Consequently, Adam's body was designed to be the vehicle through which he would relate to the material world that God created for him. However, the reality of his identity was not defined by the clay form of his body, but by the image of his Maker within it.

Adam's Unique Presence:

And the Lord God... breathed into his [Adam's] nostrils <u>the breath of life</u>; and man became a living being

(Genesis 2:7). What is this "breath of life" that God breathed into Adam? To begin with, God is Spirit (John 4:24) and Life, and whatever He breathes produces spirit and life. Job 32:8 confirms what the "breath of life" is. It reads, *but there is a spirit in man, And the breath of the Almighty gives him understanding*. This scripture clearly identifies the *spirit in man* as the *breath of the Almighty*, or the "breath (really spirit) of the Life-giver". Further,

the reality of his [Adam's] identity was not defined by the clay form of his body, but by the image of his Maker within it.

Proverbs 20:27 says that *the spirit of man is the lamp of the Lord, searching all the innermost parts of his being*. In other words, the spirit of man is the light of God's presence in him. Here is another very enlightening scripture:

> ...*Thus says the Lord, who stretches out the heavens, lays the foundation of the earth, and forms the spirit of man within him*:
>
> Zechariah 12:1

Just as God formed the body of humankind from the dust of the ground, God formed Adam's spirit from His very own Spirit. It is this extended presence of God's Spirit in Adam that reproduced in him the image and likeness of his Creator. God's own image (nature) was imprinted in the spirit of the first human, Adam. It was this spirit-imprint that gave Adam the ability to be godlike in character and outward expression and behavior. God's design was that Adam's understanding of himself and his environment should come from his spirit-union with his Creator.

It is of critical importance for every reader of this

book to understand that God's order of operation, or default setting, in humanity was for His spirit in Adam—the first human—to be the source of his life, and the well-spring of his every thought, word and action. His spirit-image in Adam predisposed him to be godlike in all his expressions. God never intended Adam's life to be governed directly by his brain function, but by his spirit-image. His brain function was intended to be the servant of his spirit-image, and not its master. This was and still is God's default setting in humanity.

Always remember, Adam's life did not begin with his lifeless brain in his lifeless body, but by the spirit from the living God that was breathed into him. *And the Lord God... breathed into his [Adam's] nostrils the breath of life; and man **became** a living being* (Genesis 2:7, emphasis mine). Adam **became** only because God **breathed**, and not because Adam's body had a brain in it. Without God's spirit Adam's body was only a house with no one living in it. Ponder this irrefutable truth: You are, and I am, ONLY because God is. Whether we choose to believe that or not, whether we acknowledge God or not, this is the reality. We cannot breathe for one moment without some measure of His presence in us. We are all some derivative of God's Spirit-life.

...God's default setting in humanity was for His spirit in Adam... to be the source of his life, and the well-spring of his every thought, word and action.

However, we must examine God's "order of operation" in humanity more closely. God breathed, and Adam became a living or self-conscious being. Before this breath, the clay form of Adam's body had a brain, but absolutely no mind; because mind is not a physical element of our existence but a spiritual element. When God's spirit of life connected with Adam's lifeless brain immediately Adam became alive or self-conscious of his existence. His brain did not only respond to God's spirit, but also communicated life to his entire body, and the body responded to his brain as well, making Adam a functioning, cohesive unit. Adam's body became the vehicle for the physical expression of his **soul**—*the internal, invisible and two-way communication between his spirit and his brain.*

*Adam **became** only because God **breathed**, and not because Adam's body had a brain in it. Without God's spirit Adam's body was only a house with no one living in it.*

Please do not rush over or miss this perfect "order of operation" God established in His infinite wisdom. It did not begin with the human brain and its thinking, but with God's Spirit and His breathing, forming Adam's spirit image and identity in his lifeless body (Zechariah 12:1). In other words, God established His point of contact with humanity in His spirit-life that He shared with the race through its first ancestor, Adam. Adam's spirit (God's Life in him) was designed to rule over the activities of his brain and his body, directing the communication and the expression of both.

Ponder this irrefutable truth: You are, and I am, ONLY because God is.

In like manner, and as the servant to his spirit, Adam's brain was to govern the activities and expressions of his body. As was mentioned earlier, this was Adam's default setting, designed to facilitate a consistent, enduring relationship with his Creator. Just as a cellphone or computer has a default setting installed by its manufacturer to give a consistent response every time it is booted on, so God intended to have an unbroken, unfailing relationship with humanity via the default setting He installed in the human race.

Although there is no simple way to give a graphic portrayal that would adequately illustrate God's "order of operation" in humanity, figure 1 below represents my candid attempt to do so. The power of influence and the "order of operation" governing the spirit, brain and body are illustrated by the movement from the dominant, thick, solid line to the most subservient, thin, broken line. Firstly, from God's Spirit to His spirit-image in humanity (Adam), then from the human spirit to the brain, and from the brain to the body. There is also the response relationship that flows in the opposite direction—the body communicating with the brain, the brain with the human spirit, and the human spirit with God's Spirit. Notably, the Driver of the entire operation is the Spirit of the Creator, and the final response to God's action is the obedience of the human body.

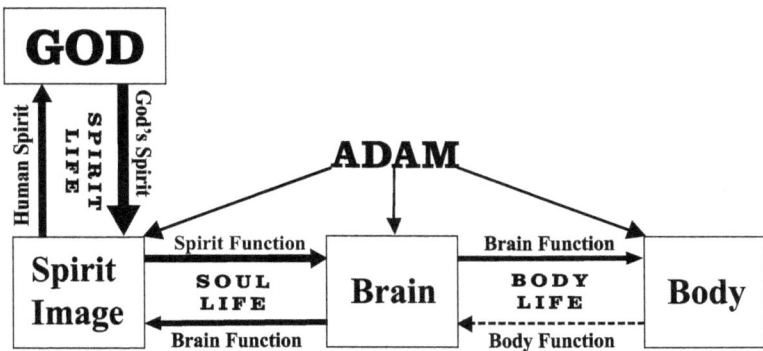

Simplified Schematic of God's Order of Operation in Humanity
Fig. 1

Key:
- God's Spirit inducing and influencing Adam's spirit.
- Adam's spirit responding to God's Spirit & also influencing his brain.
- Adam's brain responding to his spirit & also influencing his body.
- - - - Adam's body responding to and sending information to his brain.

By breathing His **spirit** into Adam, God created humanity's *God-consciousness*—Adam's awareness of God's presence and influence; by Adam's **soul** (the inner communication between the spirit and the brain), He initiated humanity's *self-consciousness*—Adam's awareness of his existence; and by his physical **body**, God established Adam's *world-consciousness*—his location in, and interaction with, time and space.

The eternal God NEVER violates His "order of operation." His communication with humanity is first and foremost through His spirit-image in humanity—Spirit to spirit. It is God's spirit in humanity (often referred to as sub-consciousness by modern science) that brings awareness to the human soul and affects or directs the actions of the body. Hence, humanity was pre-ordained to be the spirit-dominant representation of the God Who created Adam in His own image, after His likeness. Through this default setting, it was and still is God's purpose for **spirit life** to be the initiator of all human thought and action; **soul life** to be the receiver, interpreter and communicator of those thoughts and actions; and **body life** to be the executor of the decisions regarding the thoughts and actions of the **soul**.

It is not coincidental, therefore, that in his Apostolic blessing upon the Christian believers in Thessalonica that Paul spoke to their spirit, soul and body in the order of their preeminence, moving from the innermost (the most dominant) to the outermost (the most subservient):

> *Now may the God of peace Himself sanctify you completely; and may your whole **spirit**, **soul,** and **body** be preserved blameless at the coming of*

our Lord Jesus Christ.

1 Thessalonians 5:23

This empowering benediction has an intentional effect that highlights God's chosen point of contact with humanity—His own spirit-image or what remains of it—in dispensing His grace and goodness to all. His living spirit-presence in humanity is the first beneficiary of His blessings which are then passed on to the human intellect and finally, the physical body. However, we often miss God's blessings because we tend to start from the wrong end first—that is, the body of physical evidence; and when we do not see any, we are sadly disappointed and discouraged. We will explore this in greater detail later. For right now, it is good for us to remember that if, or when, we violate God's "order of operation" we could never arrive at God's best results for us. Wrong order always leads to wrong answer, and many are living grievous lives of sorrow, pain and affliction as a consequence.

At the dawn of creation, Adam enjoyed the blessing of living in God's "order of operation." He did not have the challenge of trying to figure out his world through intellectual reasoning. He already knew his world through the knowledge of God imbedded in his spirit. The unbroken union of Spirit with spirit was a living, dynamic channel of infinite wisdom and knowledge. Adam was able to give names to every living creature that came on the scene prior to his creation because his spirit was in perfect union with the One who created all. Humanity was not governed by intellectual reason, but by

> *...we often miss God's blessings because we tend to start from the wrong end first— that is, the body of physical evidence.*

spirit life that was rooted in the Life of God; but something went terribly wrong. The point and purpose of this book is to shed light on exactly what happened. Let's move on to how all this got started.

Be sober, be vigilant; because you adversary the devil walks about like a roaring lion, seeking whom he may devour.

1 Peter 5:8

5

Enter the Master Hacker

In this chapter, we will review how Lucifer, the master hacker—also called the old serpent, the devil and Satan—launched his hateful campaign against God and the human family. We will examine the origin of his hacking operations and the objectives of his hateful, destructive disposition. We read in the 12th chapter of the prophetic book of Revelation:

> ^{7}"And war broke out in heaven: Michael and his angels fought with the dragon; and the dragon and his angels fought, ^{8}but they did not prevail, nor was a place found for them in heaven any longer. ^{9}So the great dragon was cast out, that serpent of old, called the Devil and Satan, who deceives the whole world; he was cast to the earth, and his angels were cast out with him. ^{10}Then I heard a loud voice saying in heaven, "Now salvation, and strength, and the kingdom of our God, and the power of His Christ have come, for the accuser of our brethren, who accused them before our God day and night, has been cast down... ^{12}Therefore rejoice, O heavens, and you who dwell in them! Woe to the inhabitants of the earth and the sea! For the devil has come down

to you, having great wrath, because he knows
that he has a short time."

Revelation 12:7-10, 12

Although we do not know all the details about this war which took place in heaven, we can deduce that Satan orchestrated a mutiny among the angels against God and His Kingdom (Revelation 12:9, 10). The Bible says that the dragon and his angels (those who sided with Satan) fought against Michael (Christ) and His angels, and they were defeated. Moreover, they lost their place in heaven, for they were thrown out from the presence of God and the heavenly hosts. Interestingly, the phrase *"and the power of his Christ"* (verse 10) points back to Michael, the Commander of the angels, who gained the victory over the dragon. While the heavens rejoiced over Christ's conquest, they greatly lamented over the threatening doom that was about to break upon the inhabitants of the earth; because the evicted rebel had set his sights on taking dominion over them. Through the prophets Isaiah and Ezekiel, God has made available to us some valuable background information into the devious character and downfall of Satan.

Lucifer, the anointed, covering cherub[3], was the original name of Satan before he disgraced himself before his Maker. For reasons unknown to man, selfish pride became a part of his spirit and led him to jealousy and envy toward his Creator. He seriously miscalculated his identity, character and ability, and pursued a path that led him to challenge the authority of the Almighty. This covering cherub had so many good things going for him. He was

---

[3]Anointed, covering cherub was an exalted angel who ministered in the immediate presence of God Most High.

specially endowed with the finest that God had to offer. He was the seal of perfection, full of wisdom, perfect in beauty, a privileged Eden visitor, covered with every precious stone, gifted musician with uniquely designed vocal cords, and a covering angel in the immediate presence of God.

The prophet Ezekiel portrays this profound description of Lucifer in one of his lamentations, using as a pseudonym, the historical figure of the king of Tyre to record the fall of this once exalted angel. He wrote:

[12]"Son of man, take up a lamentation for the king of Tyre [Lucifer], and say to him, 'Thus says the Lord God:

[12]"*You **were** the seal of perfection, Full of wisdom and perfect in beauty. [13]You **were** in Eden, the garden of God; Every precious stone was your covering: The sardius, topaz, and diamond, Beryl, onyx, and jasper, Sapphire, turquoise, and emerald with gold. The workmanship of your timbrels and pipes was prepared for you on the day you were created. [14]"You **were** the anointed cherub who covers; I established you; You **were** on the holy mountain of God; You walked back and forth in the midst of fiery stones. [15]You **were** perfect in your ways from the day you **were** created, till iniquity was found in you.*

Ezekiel 28:12-15, emphasis mine

What more could anyone desire? Lucifer wanted more. Being a ministering spirit was just not enough. He wanted to be an exalted, ruling spirit. He was not satisfied with his identity. He wanted equality with God.

> [12]"How art thou fallen from heaven, O Lucifer, son of the morning! how art thou cut down to the ground, which didst weaken the nations! [13]For thou hast said in thine heart, *I* will ascend into heaven, *I* will exalt my throne above the stars of God: *I* will sit also upon the mount of the congregation, in the sides of the north: [14]*I* will ascend above the heights of the clouds: <u>I will be like the most High</u>. [15]Yet thou shalt be brought down to hell, to the sides of the pit."

Isaiah 14:12-15, KJV, emphasis mine

The five I-statements made by Lucifer in the above scripture portray his lofty, sinister ambition, and his selfish, evil spirit. Herein is the origination of sin. It is rather ironic and, at the same time, quite interesting to note that the middle letter of the words "Lucifer," "Sin" and "Pride" is the letter "I". Pride, the spirit and root of selfishness, became the insignia of the fallen angel and is a major weapon in the arsenal that he uses against mankind.

The elevation and the coronation of "the Self" has become the hallmark of our fallen race. It is no wonder there is a resurgence of I-consciousness in the everyday conversations of our present society. Everywhere "self" cries out for expression—WhatsApp, Facebook, Instagram, Snapchat, Twitter, etcetera—driving this last-day generation into the deceptive

> *The elevation and the coronation of "the self" has become the hallmark of our fallen race.*

and dangerous I-zone. Few, if any at all, are truly aware of the diabolical, unseen forces that are driving this faddish societal behavior in a forever quest for recognition and self-identification.

Can anyone explain, with any degree of clarity, how and when a Macintosh computer became an I-Mac; a simple book became an I-book; a phone became an I-phone; a music pod became an I-pod; and the tunes it plays became known as I-tunes? I was driven along a particular street in Orlando, Florida, and the nifty sign on a bakery enterprise caught my attention. It read, I-Bake. Are all these "I-tags" chance phenomena? I believe not!

Interestingly, there is no end to the I-listing as increasing numbers of people continue to create lists of their own. If one should review any search engine on the internet for "I-" attached to any letter of the alphabet, that individual will have a most amazing discovery. Who or what is really driving this I-crazed generation? God alone is the ultimate "I" and the great "I AM" because He is before all, created all, and by Him all things hold together. When Satan declared *"I will be like the Most High"* (Isaiah 14:14), he revealed the selfish ambition of his evil heart—to be another "I" in God's universe. However, there could only be one supreme "I", for there is only one God who is Sovereign over all. Imagine for a minute, a young man trying to stand as an equal to his father in his daddy's house. This is the formula for barefaced rebellion, and this is exactly what happened in heaven.

Woe to Humanity

Lucifer attempted to steal God's identity while living in God's domain, and while ministering before His presence.

However, his shameless audacity backfired because he gravely misjudged his position before his Creator. His egocentric aspiration caused him to lose his gracious standing before the Majesty of the universe and brought catastrophic

God alone is the ultimate "I" and the great "I AM" because He is before all, created all, and by Him all things hold together.

disaster upon himself and his fellow angels who chose to follow him. The Bible says that their place was no longer found in heaven (Revelation 12:8), but they were cast out of God's immediate domain.

Nevertheless, what Lucifer failed to accomplish in the courts of heaven, he was determined to perpetrate through the human family on earth. Heaven's reaction to the devil's expulsion is quite noteworthy:

> *[12]Therefore rejoice, O heavens, and you who dwell in them! Woe to the inhabitants of the earth and the sea! For the devil has come down to you, having great wrath, because he knows that he has a short time.*
>
> Revelation 12:12

Satan's wrath against God was now directed to the crowning act of His creation—the human family. The text says that the devil came to earth with raging anger because he was very much aware that he was now confined to the limited realm of time. He came with the sole intention to *steal, kill and destroy* (John 10:10) any and everything that is called God's. Masquerading himself in the wily serpent, he entered the peaceful Eden home of the first human family to execute his vengeance against his Creator. The first five verses of Genesis 3 paint a picture that gives us good insight into the devil's deadly hacking operation—his goals, objectives and tactic.

> [1]"Now the serpent was more cunning than any beast of the field which the Lord God had made. And he said to the woman, "Has God indeed said, 'You shall not eat of every tree of the garden'?" [2]And the woman said to the serpent, "We may eat the fruit of the trees of the garden" [3]but of the fruit of the tree which is in the midst of the garden, God has said, 'You shall not eat it, nor shall you touch it, lest you die.'" [4]Then the serpent said to the woman, "You will not surely die. [5]For God knows that in the day you eat of it your eyes will be opened, and you will be like God, knowing good and evil."
>
> Genesis 3:1-5, emphasis mine

Hacking Goals

Firstly, the devil did not abandon his highest ambition to be *like the Most High* (Isaiah 14:14). What he failed to accomplish in heaven he was determined to establish on earth. Since God gave Adam complete dominion over the earth and the authority to subdue it (Genesis 1:28), Satan's goal was to wrest that control away from Adam and install himself as absolute ruler of earth in Adam's place. Ultimately, the devil wanted to be God's equal on earth.

Satan's goal was to wrest... control away from Adam and install himself as absolute ruler of earth in Adam's place. Ultimately, the devil wanted to be God's equal on earth.

Secondly, Satan wanted to imprint his deceitful image and likeness in humanity so that he could sit as "God" in the human soul, guiding and directing the thoughts and actions of humanity.

Satan knew that in order to get Adam and Eve to sin he had lure them into assuming his own self-centered image and nature, the foundation of which were envy and lust. He knew quite well that sin could not occur where there is no lust. That's how sin got started with him and led to his rebellion against God. Incidentally, and most appropriately, **S.I.N.** forms the perfect acronym that depicts *S*atan's *I*mage and *N*ature. Consequently, he sought to replace God's image and nature in humanity with his own image and nature. In this way, he could establish a platform for his envious, lustful Self to be the life-spring of all human thoughts, words and actions.

> Incidentally, and most appropriately, **S.I.N.** forms the perfect acronym that depicts *S*atan's *I*mage and *N*ature.

Finally, he intended to use humanity as his platform to continue his rebellious campaign against God—to hurt his Maker by using His own creative masterpiece (humankind) to wage war against Him.

Hacking Objectives

In order to achieve his goals, the evil one set out on his deceptive scheme to hack into the human soul and unseat God as the fountain of life, thought and behavior. In a careful review of Genesis 3:1-5, one can see some of the hidden objectives of Satan as he executed his attack on the first family. The very first word out of the demonized serpent's mouth were intended to cause doubt and suspicion about

God in Eve's mind. "*[Really], has God indeed said, you shall not eat of every tree of the garden*" (Genesis 3:1, bracket mine)? The devil's question was a complete lie, loaded as a half-truth. His main objective was to portray God as a liar who was withholding good from her and her husband, robbing them of their true potential. In other words, God could not be trusted. The evil one was subtly projecting the elements of his own devious thoughts on the character of God to undermine the Creator's Personhood in Eve's mind.

Secondly, he wanted to invite conversation and push Eve to think about his loaded suggestion. Satan and those inspired by him are never after the truth, but always after achieving their evil objectives that their questions are designed to invoke. By this veiled approach, the serpent's other objective was to change Eve's state of being, and, through her, accomplish the same in Adam. He wanted to transform the holy pair from being GOD-centered, GOD-directed creatures, to SELF-centered, SELF-directed individuals; from being righteous spirits to living as sinful beings. The devil directed his attack to the very core of human existence because he understood that humanity's state of being drives all its acts of doing. He had great and unimaginably dreadful plans for them.

The devil directed his attack to the very core of human existence because he understood that humanity's state of being drives all its acts of doing.

Hacking Tactic

At the very heart of Satan's hacking plot is the reversing of the grand divine design, the changing of God's default setting[4], or "order of operation" in humanity. Even though I will deal with this in greater detail in the next chapter, I see it fit to introduce it here as a RED alert for all readers of this book, so please pay careful attention. Everything that has happened, or that is currently going on, in our lives is a byproduct of the devil's successful hacking of the human soul.

"God's order of operation" governs ALL that occurs in our lives and in this world. Since the days they were spoken, the powerful, infallible, living words of God created our world, establishing the "order of operation" in every system known to humanity. These same words have held this creation together for centuries in spite of the relentless attacks by the evil one upon their enduring legacy of trustworthiness. Disrupting and changing God's "order of operation" in humanity and the creation have been and still is the devil's road map for hacking and controlling the human race and our world. The evil one replaced God's default setting in humanity with his very own. Once God's "order of operation" is altered, chaos, confusion and calamity are the sure results. We are currently living on a planet in rebellion against its Creator and we are reaping daily the dreadful consequences as hapless victims of satanic hacking. How

> *Disrupting and changing God's "order of operation" in humanity and the creation have been and still is the devil's road map for hacking and controlling the human race and the creative environment.*

---

[4]Default setting is the original preset operational configuration established by a manufacturer for the precise functioning of a computer or an electronic device and its software. Whenever the device is turned on, it will automatically load its default setting to accomplish any task. In this book, default setting and "order of operation" are used interchangeably to refer to God's preset design of Adam and his race to function harmoniously with Him and the rest of His creation.

the evil one executed this dreadful scheme is the subject of our next chapter.

And we know that... the whole world lies under the sway of the wicked one.

1 John 5:19

6

How Satan Hacked Humanity

1"Now the serpent was more cunning than any beast of the field which the Lord God had made. And he said to the woman, "Has God indeed said, 'You shall not eat of every tree of the garden'?" 2And the woman said to the serpent, "We may eat the fruit of the trees of the garden; 3but of the fruit of the tree which is in the midst of the garden, God has said, 'You shall not eat it, nor shall you touch it, lest you die.'" 4Then the serpent said to the woman, "<u>You will not surely die</u>. 5For God knows that in the day you eat of it your eyes will be opened, and <u>you will be like God</u>, knowing good and evil." 6So when the woman <u>saw</u> that the tree was good for food, that it was pleasant to the eyes, and a tree desirable to make one wise, <u>she took of its fruit and ate</u>. She also gave to her husband with her, and he ate. 7Then the eyes of both of them were opened, and they knew that they were naked; and they sewed fig leaves together and made themselves coverings.

Genesis 3:1-7

The primary goal of any successful hacker is to take full control of an entire computer network to do whatever he desires with it—whether mere mischief, extortion, theft or even wanton destruction. This was, and is, no different for the enemy of the human soul. The Bible tells us that the devil's intention is to steal, kill and destroy (John 10:10) everything our loving Creator provided for our life and enjoyment. This chapter will reveal how the evil one pulled off the greatest hacking scheme in the history of humanity, and also the delivery system that he instituted to keep the human race in perpetual, oppressive servitude.

In the last section of the previous chapter, I hinted that the devil targeted and interfered with God's default setting in humanity, replacing it with one of his own devising. At this point, it is worth remembering that God shared the Spirit-image of His own Life with humanity not only for the first family and its generations to express the very elements of His righteous nature and character, but also as the delivery point for every gift and blessing to the human race and its earthly home. His Spirit did not only form Adam's spirit within him (Zechariah 12:1), but also gave life to Adam's brain and body. In other words, the life of the father of humanity originated with his spirit and not his lifeless brain and body-house. Interestingly, the reverse happens whenever the curse of death visits anyone of Adam's descendants. Once the spirit vacates the body-house, the residence is not only empty, but the brain that once turned on the "houselights"[5] and "utensils" is also completely dead.

Once the spirit vacates the body-house, the residence is not only empty, but the brain that once turned on the "houselights" and "utensils" is also completely dead.

---

[5] By "houselights" and "utensils" I mean body organs and their responding body parts.

In simple words, *spirit in* brings life, and *spirit out* leaves death.

Consequently, I need to reiterate that God intended His spirit in Adam to rule over the thought processes of his brain and the resulting actions and reactions of his body. This was his creative default setting for harmonious relations with his Creator and the means by with he was to execute his dominion over all creation. There was perfect union of Spirit to spirit—God's and Adam's—that informed and guided all Adam's thoughts and behaviors. A quick review of Figure 1 may be necessary at this point to keep in mind the dynamics of God's "order of operation" in humanity as we continue our journey through this book.

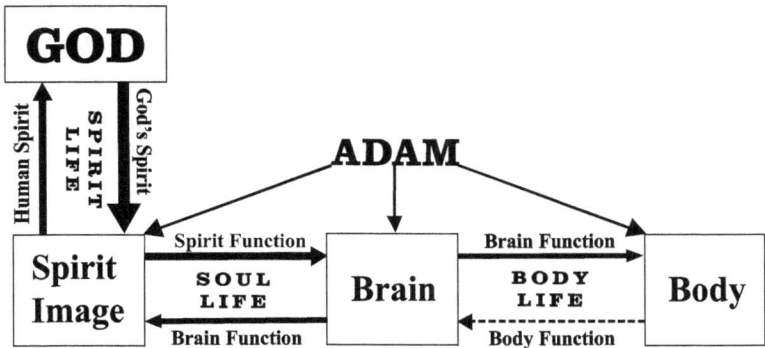

Simplified Schematic of God's Order of Operation in Humanity

Fig. 1

Key:

- God's Spirit inducing and influencing Adam's spirit.
- Adam's spirit responding to God's Spirit & also influencing his brain.
- Adam's brain responding to his spirit & also influencing his body.
- - - - Adam's body responding to and sending information to his brain.

Additionally, we have already discussed in chapter 4 that **spirit life function** represents the communication between God and His spirit image in humanity (Adam). **Soul life function** represents the communication between Adam's spirit and brain; and **body life function** represents the communication between Adam's brain and body which are both physical organs. It is also very important to remember that the body without spirit life is a dead form with a physical brain but absolutely NO mind. However, with the infusion of spirit life the dynamic organ of the soul is quickened since the "mind of the spirit"[6] is now able to communicate with the brain.

Changing God's "Order of Operation"

"Now the serpent was more subtle than any beast of the field which the LORD God had made. And he said unto the woman, Yea, <u>hath God said</u>, Ye shall not eat of every tree of the garden?"

Genesis 3:1, KJV

Now let's turn our attention to this conversation between the serpent and Eve. Satan, as the masquerading hacker, presents a question containing a deliberate half-truth (which is a whole lie) designed to evoke suspicion and doubt in Eve's mind regarding the character of God. However, the

The whole point of Satan's question was to switch God's "order of operation" to initiate a response from Eve's head rather than her spirit.

---

[6]Since God's Spirit has a mind (See Romans 8:26, 27), so does God's spirit-image in humanity (See Romans 8:6). Moreover, since Christ's Spirit and the spirit of born-again believer are one (See 1 Corinthians 6:17; Galatians 4:6), the believer also possesses the "mind of Christ" (See 1 Corinthians 2:16), although very few know how to live from that victorious place.

thrust of this question was more than an effort to paint God as a liar. The main purpose of Satan's question was to switch God's "order of operation" to initiate a response from Eve's head (or intelligent brain function) rather than her spirit. What God had said was already coded in her spirit which was in perfect union with His, but by posing a question of doubt, the devil forced Eve to think about what God had said. Wow! How crafty and diabolic! The Bible indicates that in her innocence, Eve took the bait and attempted to defend the character of God. That was noble but it was also full of corruption as we shall soon see. Eve responded:

> *2And the woman said to the serpent, "We may eat the fruit of the trees of the garden; 3but of the fruit of the tree which is in the midst of the garden, God has said, 'You shall not eat it, <u>nor shall you touch it</u>, lest you die.' "*
>
> Genesis 3:2, 3

The moment Eve responded to the devil's baited question, he promptly initiated the process of establishing control over her life, by taking her down a path of absolutely NO return. It was, and still is, never the devil's intent to discover the truth about what God said but to dethrone Him from the soul. Eve's attempted defense of God was also not completely accurate, and that opened her up to greater deception. Now what did God actually say?

> *16And the Lord God commanded the man, saying, "Of every tree of the garden you may freely eat; 17but of the tree of the knowledge of good and evil <u>you shall not eat</u>, for in the day that you eat*

of it you shall surely die."

Genesis 2:16, 17

Nowhere in his conversation with Adam did God ever say, *"nor shall you touch it,"* according to Eve's version. This one inclusion opened the door for deception, for it was possible that the serpent was already touching the tree and obviously was not dead. Eve had no idea as to when she transitioned from the realm of faith in God to the whole new world of human logic and the rule of the physical senses over spirit life in her soul. Hence, the master hacker pressed his claim by offering her some more intellectual stimulation:

> ..."You will not surely die. *5For God knows* that *in the day you eat* of it *your eyes will be opened*, and *you will be like God*, knowing good and evil."

Genesis 3:4, 5

Eve was seduced into the realm of human logic from which the evil one would not allow her to retreat or escape. Thus, he repeated God's words back to her, but with one little inclusion of his own, *"not"*. God said, *"you will surely die,"* but the serpent said, *"you will not surely die."* In other words, "do not trust what God said to you, trust your own intelligence and your senses because God is holding something back from you. Satan again repeated God's own words back to her, but once more with his own deceptive twist: *"for*

Eve had no idea when see transitioned from the realm of faith in God to the whole new world of human logic and the rule of the physical senses over spirit life in her soul.

He knows that in the day you eat of it your eyes will be opened, and you will be like God [BUT I WILL BE THE ONE CONTROLLING YOU]⁷, knowing good and evil" (bracket, my inclusion).

This is just simply amazing. Eve heard very clearly *"you will be like God."* What she did not hear was the very real, but unspoken, wicked intention of the evil one, *"but I will be the one controlling you."* Needless to say, she was completely outdone. Her spirit was completely neutralized throughout the conversation. She entertained the possibilities of a better existence and allowed her imagination to design a future which she thought she did not have, but that was already a reality that she was experiencing in her spirit from the day of her creation. Truthfully, Eve was already like God in her spirit-image since she was created as an extension of His own life. She also had perfect knowledge since she had a direct link to the fountain of all wisdom and knowledge. Eve was totally hacked, and the Bible records her dreadful, self-centered decision:

> *Eve was seduced into the realm of human logic from which the evil one will not allow her to retreat or escape.*

> *⁶So when the woman <u>saw</u> that the tree was good for food, that it was pleasant to the eyes, and a tree desirable to make one wise, <u>she took of its fruit and ate</u>. She also gave to her husband with her, and he ate.*
>
> Genesis 3:6

Please pay attention to the word "saw" in the above

---

⁷These words were not actually spoken by the serpent but represent my personal inference of the unspoken intention of the evil one.

text. This is not a reference to physical vision, but logical, human calculation. Eve made a logical deduction of all that the devil said, and it made sense to her based upon what she was then seeing and envisioning. Herein lies the birthplace of human logic, and the rise of human intelligence over the voice of God in the human spirit (often referred to as conscience or innate consciousness). This is the same principle at work in every human being every time a person chooses to act contrary to the voice of God expressed through the organ of his conscience.

In the very act of musing upon and heeding the hacker's lies, Eve was not only changing forever God's default setting in herself, but also her state of being and her grasp of reality. She trusted her external senses more than inner spirit, and in so doing disassociated and swapped God's image—the very core of her existence—to define herself by only what could be perceived in the physical realm. Consequently, her intellect and physical body with its senses became the new reality of her total existence. This is the driver of the devil's hacking operation and the oppressive source of every human woe. I will expand on this sad, insidious reality as we continue the conversation in this volume.

However, let me hasten to say that Eve made four grave mistakes in her downward spiral into a life of disgraceful bondage. By sharing these, it is my hope that every reader of this work would gain insights into his own decision-making process and be able to avert disastrous behaviors and their dreadful consequences.

> *In the very act of musing upon and heeding the hacker's lies, Eve was not only changing forever God's default setting in herself, but also her state of being and her grasp of reality.*

1. ***Eve entertained a conversation with the devil.*** Conversation with the evil one or any of his agents is never a profitable exercise for a child of God, because the devil is never after truth. He is a liar, and the father of all lies. How many of us have made the dreadful mistake of answering a loaded, but seemingly innocent, question that resulted in very explosive arguments or even worse, nasty fights and unnecessary injury? The trouble for most is that they are unable to detect the spirit of the evil one in their human counterpart, be that family, friend or foe. REMEMBER the innocent serpent was the speaking devil!

2. ***Eve thought she could have cleared the name of God before the wily serpent***. I label this well-intended act corrupt nobility. God does not need any created being to defend Him. He is more than capable of defending Himself against all that He has created. Many who take upon themselves to be apologists for God are making the same sad mistake of Eve. They are being woefully deceived. The evil one or his emissaries cannot be convinced by truth. Only those who are of the Truth are capable of hearing and receiving the truth. Jesus once told Pilate, the Roman Governor, *I have come into the world, to testify to the truth. Everyone who is of the truth hears My voice* (John 18:37). Christ never defended the Father. He spoke only

her [Eve's] intellect and physical body with its senses became the new reality of her total existence. This is the driver of the devil's hacking operation...

as the Father, Himself, would (John 12:49, 50). In this regard, John, the beloved disciple, wrote: *We are of God. He who knows God hears us; <u>he who is not of God does not hear us</u>. By this we know the spirit of truth and the spirit of error* (1 John 4:6, emphasis mine). Beware of the corrupt pride associated with being labeled a defender of God.

3. ***Eve placed her intelligence and senses above the presence of God in her spirit.*** She substituted faith in God with her human logic in her response to Satan, who deliberately held her attention on that platform (logic) until he secured all that he wanted. She was successfully hacked.

4. ***Eve yielded to the lusts that the evil one awakened in her through his artful suggestion***. A careful reading of Genesis 3:6 above reveals what these lusts are in their order: (a) *"...when the woman saw that the tree was good for food"* speaks to the lust of the flesh or physical satisfaction. (b) *"...that it was pleasant to the eyes"* speaks to the lust of the eyes or visual desire (the window-shopping syndrome). (c) *"...a tree desirable to make one wise"* speaks to the lust of self-importance, also known as self-pride. Satan craftily created his own lustful image and nature (S.I.N.) in Eve to desire what she was misled to believe she did not already possess—the image and likeness of God. The moment this deadly incursion occurred, Eve's righteous nature and outlook were permanently changed, and she became a self-centered, polluted soul. Immediately, she began to function from that compromised identity and disposition

and a false, inverse reality in which the physical appears more real than the spiritual. Thus, *when the woman saw that the tree was good for food, that it was pleasant to the eyes, and a tree desirable to make one wise, she took of its fruit and ate. . .* Genesis 3:6.

The picking and eating of the fruit were only the mere results of her newly acquired sinful state of being that prompted and satisfied the lusts it evoked from her darkened soul. The Bible states very clearly, *[14]But each one is tempted when he is carried away and enticed by his own lust. [15]Then **when lust has conceived, it gives birth to sin;** and when sin is accomplished, it brings forth death* (James 1:14, 15, NASB, emphasis mine). Most certainly, lust was conceived in Eve and gave birth to her sinful actions. Later on, I will show how the devil continues to use the same three lusts to entice, entrap and control humanity.

Separation from the Life of God

[17]This I say, therefore, and testify in the Lord, that you should no longer walk as the rest of the Gentiles walk, in <u>the futility of their mind</u>, [18]having their <u>understanding darkened</u>, being <u>alienated from the life of God</u>, because of the ignorance that is in them, because of the blindness of their heart.

Ephesians 4:17, 18

The moment after *S*atan's *I*mage and *N*ature (S.I.N.)

were created in Eve," her spirit broke union with God and she became a sinful creature, driven by her carnal thoughts, but cut off from the Life, wisdom and knowledge of God. Even though Eve imagined herself to be wiser because of the exhilaration she must have felt through her newly discovered self-dependence, her spiritual understanding was darkened because she was separated from the Source of Light. Armed with blissful excitement, she became a powerful tool of the evil one to orchestrate the downfall of her husband.

Somehow Eve was able to persuade her husband to follow her lead in violating God's command regarding the tree of the knowledge of good and evil. Consequently, Adam broke rank with his Creator, partook of the fruit and sealed the fate of his future generations. It is also very important to note that Adam's decision to eat of the forbidden fruit was not the result of the serpent's artful deception, but one of willful disobedience towards God, through listening to the voice of his wife. God later commented to him, *"...Because you have heeded the voice of your wife, and have eaten from the tree of which I commanded you, saying, 'You shall not eat of it': "Cursed is the ground for your sake; in toil you shall eat of it all the days of your life"* (Genesis 3:17). The Apostle Paul also confirms that *"...Adam was not deceived, but the woman being deceived, fell into transgression"* (1 Timothy 2:14).

Whatever Adam's reason was for obeying the voice of his wife, it followed the very same path as Eve's. He violated His Creator's "order of operation" coded in him and elevated human logic above the echo of God's voice in his spirit. Adam, not Eve, was the

> *Adam's decision to eat of the forbidden fruit was not the result of the serpent's artful deception, but one of willful disobedience towards God.*

devil's primary target because he carried the seeds of the entire human race in his loins. Eve, and every woman after her, was designed to be the receiver of those seeds, not the "producer" of them. By his single act of disobedience, the father of humanity severed his union with God and plunged his future generations into a life of demonic slavery that marches everyone to physical and eternal death—complete separation from the Life of God. Sadly, the image and nature of God were supplanted and overruled by the image and nature of the evil one and became the permanent legacy of Adam to the human race.

Consequently, the Scriptures clearly state that *in Adam all die* (1 Corinthians 15:22), and that *through one man [Adam] sin entered the world, and death through sin, and thus death spread to all men, because all sinned* (Romans 5:12, bracket mine). All sinned when Adam sinned because Adam carried all of humanity in himself; so, all die as the very tragic result. Satan succeeded in his plan of hacking the very source of human existence upon the earth, forever changing God's default setting in humanity, replacing it with a viral operation of his own. By this infectious hack, he usurped the dominion over the earth, Adam, and his descendants, and established himself as the ruler of this age (2 Corinthians 4:3). The damage was done. Satan's virus in Adam was destined to reproduce the same negative, pernicious effects in his generations. Here is the very sad record:

> ¹*This is the book of the genealogy of Adam. In the day that God created man, He made him <u>in the likeness of God</u>. ²He created them male and female, and blessed them and called them Mankind in the day they were created. ³And*

Adam lived one hundred and thirty years, and begot [fathered] a son in his own likeness, after his image, and named him Seth.

Genesis 5:1-3

From the above scripture, we see that Adam and Eve were the only two humans who were *created* by God in His own image and after His likeness. Every other human was *born* (begotten or fathered) in the marred image and likeness of fallen Adam, since he and Eve did not produce any children prior to breaking their spirit-union with their Creator. It is simply eye-opening to note that after Adam's willful rebellion against his Maker that God referred to him as mere dust — *"dust you are, and to dust you shall return"* (Genesis 3:19). Adam's identity and life were no longer defined by God's spirit within him but by the distorted imaginations of his own sinful soul. This is the viral legacy that Adam left his future generations and its damaging, deadly effects are readily seen in the growing manifestation of evil, rebellion and corruption in our modern age.

The really tragic truth about the devil's hack of humanity is that the masses of people that roam the earth are oblivious to the fact that they have been hacked, and that they are willing participants in the destructive schemes of the evil one against their Creator and their own souls. This scenario holds true for all classes of people in our world, totally independent of personal prejudices, orientations, opinions or ideas. There is a virus in humanity that predisposes all to deceitful, corrupt and unbecoming thoughts and behaviors, and many who mistakenly succumb to the idea that they have total control of their earth-walk are often surprised by their gross miscalculations and moral indiscretions. Indeed, wise King Solomon was right when he wrote, *"Every way of man is right in his own eyes, but the Lord weighs the heart"* (Proverbs 21:2), *and "there is a way that seems right to a man, but its end is the way of death"* (Proverbs 16:25).

Adam's identity and life were no longer defined by God's spirit within him but by the distorted imaginations of his own sinful soul.

Satan's Default Setting in Humanity

As a direct result of Satan replacing God's "order of operation" with his own default setting, the spirit-image of the Creator in humanity became flawed because of its separation from His Spirit and Life. God's light in the human soul went out and the thoughts governing the mind became very dark and destructive. The Bible says that *the human spirit is the lamp of the Lord that sheds light on one's inmost being* (Proverbs 20:27, NIV); and Jesus once said that if that light in one's soul becomes dark, how great indeed is that darkness! (Matthew 6:23). In agreement, Paul said that the human understanding became darkened, ignorance replaced true knowledge, and spiritual blindness clouded human judgement.

17So I tell you this, and insist on it in the Lord, that you must no longer live as the Gentiles [unbelieving] do, in the <u>futility of their thinking</u>. 18They are <u>darkened in their understanding</u> and separated from the life of God because of the <u>ignorance that is in them</u> due to the <u>hardening of their hearts</u>. 19Having <u>lost all sensitivity</u>, they have given themselves over to sensuality so as *to indulge in every kind of impurity, and they are full of greed.*

Ephesians 4:17-19, NIV, brackets and emphasis mine

Figure 2 below gives a brief summary of Satan's replacement "order of operation" in humanity. Again, I am sharing the revelation given to me regarding this mysterious phenomenon. Through the deadly virus of SELF-life, Satan replaced God as the prevailing influence in human life and thought. Most notable in the illustration is that there is no direct link between God and His image in Adam's SELF-life, making the remnant of spirit-life in Adam weak and vulnerable to the influence of soul and body life.

Consequently, the heavy solid lines show how the devil short-circuited God's authority and influence over human life by giving the human brain and body function ascendancy over what remains of God's [8]marred spirit image in mankind. Please note that the order of dominance in Figure 2 is now the reverse to that of Figure 1. The influence of the marred human spirit-image is now a thin broken line, while the lines showing the influence of the brain and body are thick and unbroken. Also notice that the brain function now holds sway over the body and the body over the marred spirit-image of humanity. The ultimate effect of this hack was that carnal, soul life, with the help of her sister, body life, became the ruling disposition of humanity.

---

[8]Marred means disconnected from the Life of God and oppressed by corrupt soul and body life.

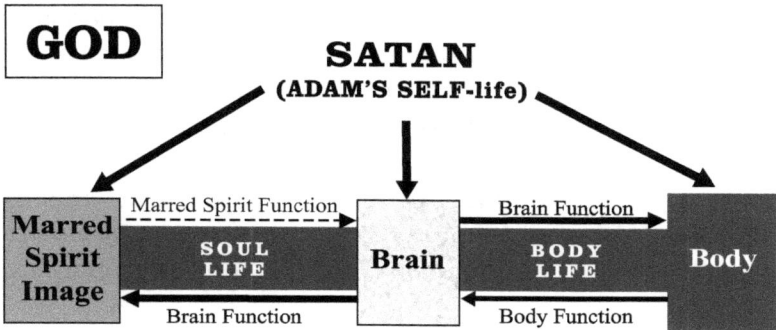

Satan's Replacement Order of Operation in Humanity
Fig. 2

Key:

- Satan's dominant influence over brain, body and marred spirit image via the human SELF.
- Brain's dominant influence over body and marred spirit image.
- Body's dominant influence over the marred spirit image.
- - - Disconnected and marred spirit image.

This dramatic change of God's order is the driving force for all the negative, harrowing experiences of the human race and of our world today. Through subtility, the spiritual default setting in humanity was changed without the active knowledge of the human instrument. Humanity was reprogramed to operate from the intellect first in all decision-making and action, minimizing, and, in most cases, neutralizing God's influence through His marred spirit-image in soul. This is the most chilling effect of satanic hacking—the blind ignorance of human beings of what's really in them. It can be likened to someone changing the default setting in a computer or cellphone and reprogramming it to operate contrary to the intent of the manufacturer. The computer or cellphone does not know that its operating system has been re-written, but just carries out the new commands of its altered setting. However, as in the case of mathematical science, whenever one violates the "order of operation" of an established system, the results are never good, even if for a while they may appear so in one's eyes.

As we continue to unveil Satan's plot against humanity, the next chapter will give us some insight as to what the devil's virus in humanity really is and how it operates.

"And I will put enmity between you and the woman, and between your seed and her Seed; He shall bruise your head, And you shall bruise His heel."

Genesis 3:15

7

Understanding the Virus in Humanity

Shortly after His baptism and the launching of His kingdom ministry, Jesus performed His first miracle at a wedding in Cana of Galilee where He converted water into wine. Because of this and the many other wonderful things He did for the masses, His name and fame were being noised abroad throughout the region around Lake Galilee. Multitudes were flocking to see and hear Him. However, Jesus never allowed Himself to be drawn in by the demands or praises of the people. He understood very clearly His earthly mission and the nature of the people He was sent to save. These two facts are very evident in this very startling statement that disciple John made about Him during His first Passover visit in Jerusalem after His notable miracle in Cana.

> *23Now when He was in Jerusalem at the Passover, during the feast, many believed in His name when they saw the signs which He did. 24But Jesus did not commit Himself to them, because He knew all men [humanity], 25and had no need that anyone should testify of man [humanity], for He knew what was in man [humanity].*
>
> John 2:23-25, brackets and emphasis mine

Through the above scripture, John gives us not only an insight into the character and personality of Jesus, but also the revelation that Jesus possessed a very thorough knowledge of humanity that struck at the very core of human existence. The text says that Jesus refused to endear Himself to those who believed in Him because He knew that there was an element of weakness (demonic virus) in humanity that predisposes every human being to be deceitful and untrustworthy. He knew quite well that many who were touting His praises and pressing into His presence would be demanding His crucifixion later. Humanity is kind and cruel in this way. Jesus *knew all men [humanity]* and had absolutely no desire to receive glory from them (human beings) for *He knew what was in man [humanity]*.

This is very heavy stuff, and quite enough to give everyone reading this book serious pause. Beyond the shadow of a doubt, there is something radically deceitful and anti-God living in all of us that forms the amoral, bankrupt fabric of human nature. The goal of this chapter is to seek to unravel what this viral element really is and to introduce God's anti-virus for overriding or even cancelling its deadly effects.

there is something radically deceitful and anti-God living in all of us that forms the amoral, bankrupt fabric of human nature.

What is this Destructive Virus in Humanity?

The answer to this very important question lies in a close re-examination of the fall of humanity and, in particular, the devil's goal of replacing God's "order of operation" in mankind with his alternative operating system. As we have already seen in chapter 6, the devil launched an attack on God's character by presenting Eve with a baited question to force her into the realm of human reason. Once Eve ventured an answer to the hacker's question, she opened the door to demonic deception, facilitated by the combined influences of her physical senses and intellectual reasoning. By encouraging her to ignore the voice of her Creator in her spirit in order to follow her carnal lusts, Satan was able to switch God's default setting (spirit-image over human reason) in her and used her as an accomplice against her husband, Adam. As a direct result, self-centeredness and human reason gained ascendency over the image of God that previously ruled human existence.

However, this was only the tip of the iceberg of the human woes that were soon to follow. The moment the holy pair severed their spirit union with God for the mirage of an existence apart from Him, the true reality of their predicament became very clear to them. Immediately, the foreign elements of fear and guilt flooded their corrupt souls. The fearful fruit of self-preservation—how to preserve their lives while separated completely from the Source of life—became the centerpiece of human existence. Suddenly, Adam and Eve found themselves in the very stressful position where all of their life's forces were instinctively directed to preserving themselves against the forces of decay and death precipitated by the curse of sin. Instantaneously, the concept of time became not only an uncompromising master of human existence and activity, but a formidable enemy of humanity as well—often referred to as a "thief". There is never enough of it (time) because degradation and death are inevitable realities facing everything in the world.

From the moment of the fall, self-preservation

and self-centeredness became the permanent drivers for all human thought and behavior. Satan had cemented his presence in the human soul through his "catch-22[9] virus" of the SELF-life—self-preservation, self-determination, self-empowerment, self-promotion and self-actualization. The sad truth is that everything that is self-driven breathes life or SELF-existence into the evil one and strengthens his hold on the human soul.

Intrinsically, SELF, really, is Satan sitting like "God" in the human soul, influencing its thoughts and behaviors in a work of rebellion and resistance against God. It (SELF) is the expression of **S**atan's **I**mage and **N**ature (S.I.N. disposition) through human life. Unknown to the masses, this is exactly what the natural human nature really is. The Bible supports this truth when it states that *"The one who does what is sinful **is of the devil**, because the devil has been sinning from the beginning. . ."* 1 John 3:8, NIV, emphasis mine. The clause **"is of the devil"** is just another way of saying is of **S**atan's **I**mage and **N**ature. It is Satan's state of being (S.I.N.) in humanity that produces all the acts of sin by humanity.

It is Satan's state of being (S.I.N.) in humanity that produces all the acts of sin by humanity.

What Lucifer failed to accomplish in heaven—to be *like the Most High* (Isaiah 14:14)—he succeeded in perpetrating in the soul of humanity on earth. Consequently, the exaltation and empowerment of the SELF is the hallmark or hacking virus of Satan's treachery against God. It forms the very heart of the devil's lie, *"you will be like God, knowing good and evil"* (Genesis 3:5). Moreover,

---

[9]Oxford Dictionary: Catch-22 is a dilemma or difficult circumstances from which there is no escape because of mutually conflicting or dependent conditions.

it fosters separation from the Creator while, at the same time, challenges every element of His sovereignty and authority. This deceptive and destructive virus of the SELF is strengthened and supported by intellectual stimulation which further promotes the pride associated with self-dependence and God-avoidance. It is no wonder then that Jesus called out denial

> *The sad truth is that everything that is self-driven breathes life or SELF-existence into the evil one and strengthens his hold on the human soul.*

of the SELF-life as the very first step that must be taken by anyone desirous of being His disciple. This call is, in truth and in fact, a daily denial of Satan.

> Then he said to them all, *"If anyone desires to come after Me, let him deny himself, and take up his cross <u>daily</u>, and follow me."*
>
> Luke 9:23

Manifestations of the Infective SELF-life Virus

From the moment the evil one succeeded in altering God's "order of operation" in humanity, there were immediate adverse manifestations in the life experience of Adam and Eve. A careful review of the Genesis 3 narrative gives us a fair overview of these negative outcomes, but their far-reaching viral effects will be dealt with in greater details later. Let's take a look at five symptoms of Satanic hacking.

> *SELF, really, is Satan sitting like "God" in the human soul...*

Symptom #1 – Human Logic (Reason) replaced Spirit-image Knowing:

> *⁶So when the woman <u>saw</u> that the tree was <u>good</u> <u>for food</u>, that it was <u>pleasant to the eyes</u>, and a tree <u>desirable to make one wise</u>, she took of its fruit and ate. She also gave to her husband with her, and he ate.*
>
> Genesis 3:6, emphasis mine

Through masterful deception, Satan succeeded in severing the dynamic union between God and His spirit-image in humanity. The free flow of knowledge and wisdom about everything from God to His children was cut off completely. The SELF-life virus in humanity drove Adam to choose independence from God at an enormous, incalculable cost. It placed him and his descendants in a very dark place, which the Word of God describes as,

> *¹⁷[walking about] in the <u>futility of their</u> <u>mind [natural intelligence]</u>, ¹⁸having their <u>understanding darkened</u>, being <u>alienated from</u> <u>the life of God</u>, because of <u>the ignorance that is</u> <u>in them</u>, because of <u>the blindness of their heart</u> <u>[disconnected spirit-life]</u>.*
>
> (Ephesians 4:17-18, brackets and emphasis mine)

The above scripture reflects an exceedingly sad state of affairs. Because of alienation from God's life and light, the human mind is futile because the understanding is dark. This estrangement from the Wellspring of all knowledge and wisdom produced gross ignorance and

the exaltation and empowerment of the SELF is the... hacking virus of Satan's treachery against God.

blindness in humanity. Satan's hack had caused irreparable damage in the human soul, and there was absolutely no going back from this disadvantageous position because the dominance of clouded human logic became a "necessary evil" for mere survival. Abiding fear of lack, physical degeneration and death became very real. For the first time Adam and Eve were compelled to use their intelligence and all their life's forces in "any way possible" in order to avert sorrow, pain and untimely demise.

Before this, Adam never faced the difficult task of trying to figure out how to sustain his life, or how to govern his once harmonious, peaceful domain. These tasks were the natural outgrowth of the flow of God's boundless life, knowledge and wisdom already in Adam's spirit-image. However, the moment this SELF-virus entered Adam, the self-perceived thinking of the "end justifying the means" became the very real, expedient mode of human operation. Consequently, logical reasoning grew out of the need for humankind to sustain a life that was once connected to the endless life and wisdom of God. The devil had succeeded in offsetting God's order and His appointed way of knowing through His unbroken union with His spirit-image in humanity. Thus, logical reasoning became humanity's survival mechanism to preserve SELF-life from all the fears associated with its separation from the life of God.

Self-preservation—really, disconnection from God's life—by its very nature consigned humanity to live in the realm of compromised human reason, which gave rise to a much greater existential dilemma. It created the perpetual need of searching for, and investigation of, information on every and any thing that could promote and preserve SELF-life. As a direct result of these ceaseless activities, the race became more imbedded in human intelligence and less connected to the now impaired image of God's presence in the human spirit. Consequently, logical reasoning, fed by the natural senses, became and remains the default mechanism for all human investigation and problem solving, and the vehicle for determining truth from error. However, intellectual reasonings, without spiritual direction, are only mere expressions of the musings of a captured, corrupt soul.

Of even greater consequence is the fact that self-preservation imperiled the ability of Adam and his future generations to exercise genuine faith and trust in God. This is a major fallout of the "catch-22"[10] SELF-life that creates a formidable barrier against God's response to the hack of humanity, and the sharing of the Good News He designed to support that response. The bedrock article of this Good News say that *without faith it is impossible to please Him, for he who comes to God must believe that He is [not was]...* (Hebrews 11:6, bracket and emphasis mine), and human logic strikes at the very heart of this truth. Many countless thousands who have come to Him find it very difficult to believe Him, that *He is* truly in their every situation working out His purpose for them. The landscape of Christianity is dotted

logical reasoning, fed by the natural senses, became and remains the default mechanism for all human investigation and problem solving, and the vehicle for determining truth from error.

profusely with "believing" unbelievers, whose daily living do not match their profession of faith in God and His Messiah—Jesus Christ. What a tangled web the enemy of our souls has weaved to keep humanity in a state of spiraling fear,

[10]Ibid, 84.

doubt and confusion.

Symptom #2 - Physical Perception replaced Actual Reality:

> *⁷Then the eyes of both of them were opened,*
> *and they knew that they were naked; and they*
> *sewed fig leaves together and made themselves*
> *coverings.*
>
> Genesis 3:7, emphasis mine

It is very interesting and important to see how the serpent shifted the center of Eve's identity from her spirit to her intellect to initiate her logical reasoning. That strategic move changed her concept of reality. She was no longer directed from her internal spirit-image but influenced by external perception. Her decision to eat the fruit was based completely upon her new perception of reality

intellectual reasonings, without spiritual direction, are only mere expressions of the musings of a captured, corrupt soul.

coordinated through her intellect and her physical vision. The Bible says *"so when the woman saw that the tree was good for food, that it was pleasant to the eyes, and a tree desirable to make one wise, she took of its fruit and ate. She also gave to her husband with her, and he ate"* (Genesis 3:6, emphasis mine).

External vision validation, fueled by the desire to be wise, which the serpent spoke into her intellect, created a new reality for Eve, and she acted on it. Through the very same means, the evil one used Eve to coerce Adam to break ties with God and embrace her reality of their future. As a direct result of their rebellious actions, their whole concept of reality of themselves and their surroundings changed permanently. Regretfully, this deceptive legacy was passed on to the rest of humanity.

Consequently, when the Bible says that *the eyes of both of them were opened, and they knew that they were naked* (Genesis 3:7), it is quite evident that something precious had been broken within them. Clearly, they had lost their spiritual identity and vision and were now defining themselves totally by their physical appearance. Prior to this point, their physical body was their house-covering[11] and they could not see any nakedness. Now all that had changed, for breaking ties with God eclipsed completely their spiritual clarity and perception of reality.

Today the devil uses the very same false view of what is truthful and real—physical sensory perception wedded to internal lusts—to drive all human relations, conversations and decision-making. By distorting our concept of reality, Satan has robbed humanity of its true identity and source of power, while he operates in the realm of the unseen, true reality to sow chaos and confusion in our world. We will explore more about this in the following chapters.

Symptom #3 – Fleshly God-avoidance replaced Spiritual God-fellowship:

> *8And they heard the sound of the Lord God walking in the garden in the cool of the day, and Adam and his wife hid themselves from the presence of the Lord God among the trees of the garden.*
>
> Genesis 3:8, emphasis mine

---

[11]See Chapter 4 to review this truth about God's order in the creation of Adam.

Fear, guilt and shame forced Adam and Eve into hiding from their Creator with whom they used to enjoy intimate fellowship. These unhealthy emotions were not a part of their human psyche until the reality of their rebellious deed dawned upon them. They had absolutely no idea what to do with those emotions and resorted to the absurd option of "hiding" from the presence of the all-seeing, all-knowing God. Because of their soul blindness and logical reasoning, they envisioned God in the physical, just as they then perceived themselves, and really thought that their presence could be concealed from Him. Unknown to them, it was the very presence of God in them that produced their sense of guilt and shame.

Many try desperately to shut out this presence of God by numbing themselves with mind-altering drugs, while other resort to God-deniability.

This scenario plays out every day in our present world. Sinners think they can hide from God when they use the cover of darkness to perpetrate their evil deeds. Somewhere in their thinking they believe they will not be seen by anyone, when, in reality, the presence of God is already at work in their spirit-conscience condemning their actions, even though they willfully ignore its promptings. Many try desperately to shut out this presence of God by numbing themselves with mind-altering drugs, while others resort to God-deniability—trying to convince themselves that God does not exist. However, the unwelcome truth is that as long as a person is living and breathing there is some measure of God's presence expressing itself within and keeping the brain and vital organs alive.

The Bible says that even those who do not acknowledge God *show the work of the law [transcript of God's presence] written in their hearts [mind], their* **conscience** *[God's active presence in the marred human spirit-image] also* <u>bearing witness</u>, *and between themselves their thoughts* <u>accusing</u> *or else* <u>excusing</u> *them* (Romans 2:15, brackets and emphasis mine). Additionally, in the first epistle of John, the apostle wrote that *"if our heart [God's presence through the voice of conscience] condemns us,* <u>God is greater than our heart, and</u> <u>knows all things</u>. *Beloved, if our heart does not condemn us,* <u>we have confidence toward God</u>" (1 John 3:20, 21, brackets and emphasis mine).

SELF-life virus in humanity hates the feeling of fear, guilt and the sense of condemnation, and will do anything to protect or preserve itself from the same.

The sad reality is that the SELF-life virus in humanity hates the feeling of fear, guilt and the sense of condemnation, and will do anything to protect or preserve itself from the same. This is one of the two major contributors that make natural humanity so God-averse. The other is the negative evil projections about God's character upon fallen, struggling human beings by the evil one and his self-righteous emissaries. Many who profess to be followers of God proclaim a "bad news" gospel that portrays God as being against sinners, waiting to execute judgement upon them. This is so far from the truth which says that God has already reconciled or made peace with the world of sinners, but the world does not even know it, and many professed Christians fail to proclaim it. Here is an interesting and very important scripture:

[18]*"Now* <u>all things</u> *are of God, who* <u>has reconciled</u> *us to Himself through Jesus Christ, and* <u>has</u>

given us the ministry of reconciliation [not condemnation or alienation], [19]that is, that God was in Christ reconciling the world to Himself, not imputing their trespasses to them, and has committed to us the word of reconciliation [not condemnation or alienation]."

2 Corinthians 5:18,19, brackets and emphasis mine

The very first thing we notice in this scripture is that it is written in the past tense, indicating completed acts of God. God *has reconciled*, not just those who believe in Jesus, but the world of humanity. That was the whole purpose of the cross. Christ's death was God's limitless ransom paid to recover and regenerate hacked humanity. Moreover, the text says that God has suspended sentence on all humanity (*not imputing their trespasses to them*) to give all the opportunity to hear the word of reconciliation from those who have been given the ministry of reconciliation, and function as ambassadors of Christ, not of Satan.

ALL sinners have already been reconciled through the act of God in Jesus Christ...

PLEASE notice that both the word and ministry in the above scripture are qualified by the adjective reconciliation—NOT judgment, condemnation or alienation. May I hasten to say that reconciliation is not only God's peace treaty for all humanity, but also the approach pathway to Himself, so all sinners could receive His gift of justification—acquittal from ALL sins—and His righteousness through faith in Jesus Christ. In other words, ALL sinners have already been reconciled through the act of God in Jesus Christ; but all sinners are not justified, or cleared from their sins, until by faith they receive God's gift of justification in Jesus Christ—His death and resurrected life.

This is the true Gospel of the Bible that every victim of Satan's hacking has a divine right to hear before leaving earth. God's generous act of reconciling ALL sinners to Himself forms an integral part of His victorious, overriding response to the hack of humanity that we will discuss more extensively in the next volume[12] of this two-book series.

Symptom #4 – Fear replaced Faith:

> [9]*Then the Lord God called to Adam and said to him, "*<u>*Where are you*</u>*?" *[10]*So he said, "I heard Your voice in the garden, and *<u>*I was afraid*</u>* because *<u>*I was naked*</u>*; and *<u>*I hid myself*</u>*."*

> Genesis 3:9, 10, emphasis mine

When God went looking for Adam in the Garden, it was not because He did not know where he was. The question was not really for Him, but for Adam, to provoke his SELF discovery in relations to his Maker. God already had the answer but wanted Adam to confirm his standing before Him. As it turned out, Adam was absent from his image of communal faith and fellowship with his Creator and answered from a foreign image of fear and dread that usurped the presence of God in him. Through the image of the SELF, Satan had cemented his presence in Adam to be the source of every human expression.

The Word of God informs us that *God has not*

---

[12]Ruthven J. Roy, *The ReGened Life – Humanity's Hope After the Hack*, coming soon.

given us the spirit of fear, but of power and of love and of a sound mind (2 Timothy 1:7). Fear is a foreign spirit from the evil one that engulfed the soul of humanity when Adam and Eve rebelled against God. This is not a characteristic of the life that flows from God, but from the SELF that is separated from the life of God. It is produced by guilt and condemnation and nurtured by human logic and the self-preserving spirit of the evil one. The apostle John says that *if our heart does not condemn us, we have confidence [not fear] toward God* (1 John 3:21, brackets and emphasis mine). Adam and Eve feared because they felt condemn by the spirit-image of God's life within them. The same spirit of the evil one still drives the thinking and behavior of humanity to this day and very often leads to disastrous results.

For fear of losing something considered important or precious, a person may make a rash decision and end up losing more than what he or she was trying to preserve or acquire. A young woman may yield to sexual pressure for fear of losing the young man of her dreams, or vice versa. Many times, what a person thinks would save the relationship often becomes the very thing that destroys it. People often lie for fear of losing a good reputation only to discover they have to keep on lying until they destroy the same reputation they were trying to protect. As a matter of fact, fear of things, people, places, situations and negative outcomes exists in every facet of human existence, creating a growing climate of stress and anxiety on our current world stage in spite of all our human achievements and advancement.

> *Fear is a foreign spirit from the evil one that engulfed the soul of humanity when Adam and Eve rebelled against God.*

<u>Symptom #5 – Soul and Speech Corruption replace Spirit Speech Alignment</u>:

> *[11]And He [God] said, "<u>Who told you that you were naked</u>? Have you eaten from the tree of which I commanded you that you should not eat?" [12]Then the man said, "<u>The woman whom You gave to be with me</u>, she gave me of the tree, and I ate." [13]And the Lord God said to the woman, "<u>What is this you have done</u>?" The woman said, "<u>The serpent deceived me</u>, and I ate."*

Genesis 3:11-13, brackets and emphasis mine

From the moment Adam opened his mouth, the evidence of his soul's corruption was quite obvious because his true identity was compromised. He who was designed as a spirit in a body-house was now defining himself by his body-house, "*I was naked.*" God asking the question, "*who told you that you were naked* was equivalent to saying, "*who told you that you were just clay*?" The omniscient Creator would not be fooled. He knew that a different spirit was directing Adam's speech.

Please notice that God did not ask Adam, "*how did you know you were naked?*" Rather, He asked, "*who told you...?*" This question, at first glance, appears somewhat strange since there was no other physical presence in the garden with Adam and Eve beside the lying serpent. However, on closer examination, God's query was deliberate, provocative and instructive. It suggests that someone was telling Adam things about himself from the inside while allowing Adam to believe that he was the one describing his fear, nakedness and distorted sense of reality. God's question to Adam speaks to the depth of Satan's incursion of the human soul, infecting and affecting every facet of human experience. Obviously, Adam, much like his present-day generations, was not immediately aware that his image was drastically altered, and that his thinking, speech and actions were being governed by the spirit of the god (the devil) he chose in place of his Maker.

God's follow-up question reinforced the truth that Adam was under the control of the arch-deceiver and rival of the Creator. *"Have you eaten from the tree...?"* is directly related to the confession of Adam's mouth, *"I was naked."* In other words, the consumption of the fruit from the tree of the knowledge of good and evil was a symbolic representation of Adam's surrender to the control of the spirit that led him to make that most deadly decision. In that singular choice, Adam gave the devil ownership over his own soul and sold his descendants into a life of slavery, *"for by whom a person is overcome, by him also he is brought into bondage"* (2 Peter 2:19). The apostle Paul confirmed this dreadful reality by asking this most sobering, suggestive question: *"Do you not know that to whom you present yourselves slaves to obey, you are that one's slaves whom you obey, whether of sin leading to death, or of obedience leading to righteousness"* (Romans 6:16)? In the very next chapter, he lamented over the finality of Adam's terrible decision. He wrote, *"we know that the law is spiritual; but I am unspiritual, sold as a slave to sin"* (Romans 7:14, NIV).

It is quite interesting to observe that Adam did not give a straight answer, but a self-preserving deflection that sought to pin the blame on Eve and on God, Himself: *"The woman whom You gave to be with me, she gave me of*

THE HACK OF HUMANITY

the tree, and I ate." In other words, "it was Eve's fault; and besides, if You did not give me this woman I would have never been in this predicament."

The very nature of the SELF-life virus is to refuse to take responsibility or accept accountability or judgment for any action it perpetrates. Rather, it always seeks to shift that blame to someone or something else. This viral effect was also present in Eve, evidenced by her evasive answer when God shifted the question to her. *"What is this you have done?"* or, in my words, *"why did you pressure your husband to follow you?"* Again, she also deflected and transferred the blame to the serpent and God. "It is the serpent's fault; and besides, if You did not create that serpent my husband and I would not have been in this situation."

Adam and Eve became captured surrogates for the evil one, passing on the same corrupt disposition to the human family. Consequently, while hacked humanity lives under the mistaken idea that everyone is the master of his own destiny, it is totally unaware of its helpless position as a pawn in the hands a diabolical puppet-master who, but for the mercy of God, is bent on its total destruction. Because of this unwitting ignorance, the cogent question God posed to Adam after his rebellion, begs for our undivided attention and careful consideration today. *"Who told you* the thoughts you are thinking about yourself, your situations and others are your very own?" *"Who told you* what you are about to say originated from yourself?" *"Who told you* what you are planning to do came from you?" *"Who told you* that (fill in the blanks)...?"

Who is the one that's really controlling our thoughts whenever we encounter sleepless nights and want to turn our minds off and just simply cannot? How much autonomy do we really have over what we think, say and do? Who is really directing all of these activities? The reality is, our brain and body functions are guided either by our deceptive SELF spirit (the image of evil one) or, if we are born-again believers, by the spirit of Christ (God's restored image) within us. There is absolutely no middle-ground position to stand on. Moreover, the simple truth remains that from the time of humanity's fall in Eden until now, God's resounding *"who told you..."* is still the most sobering question to challenge the human experience. There is still a way that appears right to a person, but in the end, it leads to destruction (Proverbs 16:25). Humanity still remains incapable of directing its own destiny without real help from above. (Jeremiah 10:23).

> ...from the time of humanity's fall in Eden until now, God's resounding *"who told you..."* is still the most sobering question to challenge the human experience.

It is very important to note at this point that Jesus knows exactly not only what corruption resides within humanity (John 2:24, 25), but also how to arrest and deal with it. He once addressed the wicked Jewish leaders of His day with this scathing rebuke that reflects Adam's dreadful legacy of deceit and corruption to humanity. This is what He said:

> [33]*"Make a tree good and its fruit will be good, or make a tree bad and its fruit will be bad, for a tree is recognized by its fruit.* [34]*You brood of vipers, how can you who are evil say anything good? For the mouth speaks what the heart is full of.* [35]*A good man brings good things out of the good stored up in him, and an evil man brings*

*evil things out of the evil stored up in him. ³⁶But
I tell you that everyone will have to give account
on the day of judgment for every empty word
they have spoken.*

Matthew 12:33-36, NIV, emphasis mine

Through Adam and Eve, the devil has polluted the soul tree or fountain of humanity to bring forth fruits of his demonic desires. That soul contamination is reflected in the deceptive, negative speech patterns of the human race, producing uncontrollable, hurtful disorders in the earth. Scripture cautions us about the dangers of an unbridled tongue. We read in the epistle of James, *"and the tongue is a fire, a world of iniquity. The tongue is so set among our members that it defiles the whole body, and sets on fire the course of nature; and it is set on fire by hell"* (James 3:6, emphasis mine).

In just these two short sentences, James tells a whole lot about the fallen human tongue. It would really require more than this chapter to unpack the depth of what James wrote about the tongue, so I will just give a brief summary to make the point of this section. Here are some powerful takeaways: (1) The tongue is a fire and a fire-setter at the same time, with the capability to direct the course of a person's life. (2) The tongue is a world of deception and trouble. (3) The tongue has the capacity to defile the whole person. A person may appear attractive, handsome and well liked until he or she begins to spill rotten garbage through the mouth. (4) The

Satan has already done his evil work in producing the pilot-light for the human tongue via his SELF-life virus in the captured soul.

fires produced by the tongue is lit from the pit of hell. Satan has already done his evil work in producing the pilot-light for the human tongue via his SELF-life virus in the captured soul.

Consequently, the problem is not with the tongue itself but with the condition of the soul fountain that refreshes or contaminates it. Whatever is in our heart will be made manifest through our speech. However, many continue to be deceived by the deflective, proverbial excuse of the "slip of the tongue" because self-preservation prevents them from accepting any responsibility for unrestrained fire-setting.

Invasive Virus Versus Victorious Anti-Virus

[14]So the LORD God said to the serpent: "Because you have done this, You are cursed more than all cattle, And more than every beast of the field; On your belly you shall go, And you shall eat dust All the days of your life. [15]And I will put enmity between you and the woman, And between your seed and her Seed; He shall bruise your head, And you shall bruise His heel."

Genesis 3:14, 15, emphasis mine

It is rather interesting to observe that in the storyline after the fall of Adam and Eve, God never questioned the serpent. He asked the fallen pair what they had done and they both deflected their answers; but when Eve referenced the serpent as the one who deceived her, God never ask the serpent, "what is this that you have done?" or "why have you done this?" He knew that the wicked "father of lies"

(John 8:44) would not only lie to Him; but that he would also seize that opportunity to viciously berate Him before His guilty children, in whose mind the pernicious seeds of blame were already sown.

Consequently, God did not address the wicked one with a question but stated forthrightly that he was guilty of seditious treason and pronounced a curse upon him. *"Because you have done this, you are cursed more than all cattle, and more than every beast of the field; On your belly you shall go, and you shall eat dust all the days of your life"* (Genesis 3:14). The Creator did not give Satan any room or opportunity to defend himself through crafty deflection or false accusations. He simply declared His verdict and exercised His executive authority to place an impassable limit on the devil's power over humanity. *"And I will put enmity between you and the woman, and between **your seed** and her **Seed**; He shall bruise your head, and you shall bruise His heel"* (Genesis 3:15).

Through this prophetic statement, God drew "a line in the sand" between two opposing seeds, one belonging to the devil and the other belonging to Himself in the womb of the prophetic woman. Naturally speaking, women are not the producers of seeds, men are. Women produce eggs that receive and house the seeds of men to procreate future generations. Consequently, God's declaration to the serpent had prophetic or symbolic implications that pointed to the Messianic mission of Jesus Christ. That mission included (1) Christ coming into the world through the womb of a woman (the Virgin Mary); (2) living a victorious life over Satan, sin, death and the grave; and, through the ministry of the Holy Spirit, (3) planting the seed of His victorious, resurrected life in the regenerated spirit of all who believe in, and receive,

Him as their Savior and Lord. However, I will reserve a more extensive treatment of this critical subject for the next volume[13] of this series.

In our current conversation, the seed of the serpent is the invasive virus of SELF-life directed by human intelligence and operates in opposition to God's sovereignty and authority. Further, I have likened the Seed of the woman as God's Anti-virus in the Person of Jesus Christ and His victorious spirit within every true believer. God has established enmity between these two seeds, often referred to as war between God's spirit and human flesh[14]. Paul, more than any other apostle, speaks to the antagonism between these two opposing forces at work in humanity.

the seed of the serpent is the venomous virus of SELF-life directed by human intelligence and operates in opposition to God's sovereignty and authority.

> [5]*Those who live according to the flesh have their minds set on what the flesh desires; but those who live in accordance with the Spirit have their minds set on what the Spirit desires.* [6]*The mind governed by the flesh is death, but the mind governed by the Spirit is life and peace.* [7]The mind governed by the flesh is hostile to God; it does not submit to God's law, nor can it do so. [8]Those who are in the realm of the flesh cannot please God.*

Romans 8:5-8, NIV, emphasis mine

---

[13]Ibid, 93.
[14]Flesh is a reference for sheer human intelligence, driven by the SELF-life, without any direction from God's spirit. It is characterized by self-centeredness and does everything to benefit the SELF

The above scripture explains that people who are fleshly (or self-centered) in their orientation and outlook, focus their attention on things that promote self-preservation or the SELF-life. In the ceaseless work of self-care, their minds are continuously weighed down with fear, worry and stress that actually work against their longevity. To the fleshly person, God is only a secondary reference when SELF calculates its inability to cope with what it perceives as an insurmountable situation or a problem too difficult to solve. On the other hand, the individual who is governed by the spirit-seed of Christ (God-centeredness) gives priority to the things of God that promotes life and peace, even in the midst of trouble.

Why does the text say that *the mind governed by the flesh is hostile to God; it does not submit to God's law, nor can it do so?* Here is something interesting God revealed to me one day while contemplating the meaning of the word "flesh". If we take the word FLESH and flip it around we get H SELF or Hidden Self. Flesh and SELF are one and the same thing—self-centeredness or the seed (spirit or disposition) of Satan operating like "God" in the human soul. It is this hidden disposition of the evil one that is referenced in our text. Unknown to the human subject, the devil continues his hatred and rebellion against God through the hacked soul of humanity. This is why it is impossible for self-centered people to please God. The defiant spirit of Satan will not allow anyone under its dominion the freedom to willingly submit in obedience to God. It will always drive its captured human subject to choose self before God whenever self is on the line or is

> If we take the FLESH and flip it around we get H SELF or Hidden Self. Flesh and SELF are one and the same thing.

lusting after something.

This conflict between the two seeds—flesh and spirit, virus and Anti-virus—is quite real. Paul further validates that *the flesh desires what is contrary to the Spirit, and the Spirit what is contrary to the flesh. They are in conflict with each other, so that you are not to do whatever you want* (Galatians 5:17, NIV). *He also stated that the natural man [one who is not born again of God's Spirit] does not receive the things of the Spirit of God, for they are foolishness to him; nor can he know them, because they are spiritually discerned* (1 Corinthians 2:14, brackets and emphasis mine). Is there any wonder we see such open rebellion against God, and the persistent effort on all fronts to keep Him out of the public space and discourse?

If we bring it closer to home, why do many who profess to be followers of Christ still find themselves questioning, resisting, overriding or side-stepping instructions, commands and directives from God? A big part of the answer lies in the ignorance of many Christians of how Satan's demonic hacking affects their spiritual experience. Although they have received God's Anti-virus through the victorious seed-life[15] of Jesus Christ, many have not learned how to access or utilize its cancelling and detoxifying power. Consequently, many have suffered great loss, while others still remain troubled about their current life's situations.

Unknown to the human subject, the devil continues his hatred and rebellion against God through the hacked soul of humanity.

One of the goals of this volume is to create spiritual

---

[15]All who have received Jesus Christ as Savior and Lord have been born again, not of flesh but of God's "incorruptible" spirit-seed (John 1:12, 13 and 1 Peter 1:23). For more information on this, see "Ruthven J. Roy, *Born Again: How to Maximize Your New Life in Christ* (Michigan: Rehoboth Publishing, 2012).

awareness of the devil's devices and show readers how to apply God's effective response against the virtual enemy living in the soul of humanity. As we close this chapter, let us take a brief look at some marked differences between these two seeds—flesh and spirit, virus and Anti-virus—battling over the human soul. Their manifestations are clear indicators of what spirit is really driving all human behaviors.

Through the serpent's invasive virus, the SELF is EVERYTHING; through God's Anti-virus, SELF is absolutely NOTHING. Under the virus, SELF is a relentless master; but under the Anti-virus, SELF is a crucified servant. The invasive virus in humanity declares, "I can do anything." "I am a DIY (Do It Yourself) person." God's innocuous Anti-virus says, *"I can of Mine own self do NOTHING: as I hear, I judge and my judgment is just; because I seek not mine own will, but the will of the Father which hath sent me."* (John 5:30, KJV). It is of remarkable interest to note that Jesus was never characterized by the "do it yourself" spirit that promotes human independence and self-mastery. He lived by every word of God, and always followed His Father's will.

Additionally, the venomous SELF-life virus in humanity is proud and boastful, and seeks the glory of other humans; but God's innocuous Anti-virus is humble and seeks only the glory of God. He declares: *"...learn from Me, for I am gentle and lowly in heart..."* (Matthew 11:29); *"I do not accept glory from human beings"* (John 5:41, NIV). Those who are always seeking human approval are unsuspecting victims of Satanic hacking, and often finds themselves living under the tyranny of jealousy, disappointment and emotional distress. On

> *Those who are always seeking human approval are unsuspecting victims of Satanic hacking...*

the contrary, Jesus was never disappointed by humanity, because He knew humanity, and also what was in humanity (John 2:24, 25). I hope this chapter has helped us with that understanding.

15Do not love the world or the things in the world. If anyone loves the world, the love of the Father is not in him. 16For all that is in the world—the lust of the flesh, the lust of the eyes, and the pride of life—is not of the Father but is of the world. 17And the world is passing away, and the lust of it; but he who does the will of God abides forever.

1 John 2:15-17

8

Satan's Viral Support System

At the dawn of Creation, God gave Adam and Eve the authority to exercise complete dominion over the atmospheric heaven, the earth, the seas, and all the creatures that lived in them. He said to holy pair, *"Be fruitful and multiply; fill the earth and <u>subdue it;</u> <u>have dominion </u>over the fish of the sea, over the birds of the air, and over every living thing that moves on the earth"* (Genesis 1:28, emphasis mine). However, through disobedience and rebellion against the Creator, Adam and Eve yielded their allegiance to the evil one, and by that very act turned the rulership of their domain over to him. The devil had scored a major victory, seizing control not only over humanity, but also over the earth and its environment. In this chapter, we will examine how the evil one uses his control over our world to sustain his venomous virus in humanity, in order to keep the race in bondage and continue his rebellious war against the God of the universe.

The Ruler of this World

It is rather astonishing to see how Satan gloated over his captured domain when he confronted Jesus[16] in the

---

[16] Jesus is the prophetic "Seed of the woman" (Genesis 3:15), God's Anti-virus to vanquish Satan and nullify ALL the deadly effects of his venomous virus in humanity.

wilderness of temptation. Luke's version of the encounter gives us a very clear picture of the devil's treachery.

> *⁵Then the devil, taking Him up on a high mountain, showed Him all the kingdoms of the world in a moment of time. ⁶And the devil said to Him, "All this authority I will give You, and their glory; for this has been delivered to me, and I give it to whomever I wish. ⁷Therefore, if You will worship before me, all will be Yours."*

Luke 4:5-7 emphasis mine

In the scripture, the devil is telling Jesus that earth and all its glories were handed over to him—by fallen Adam, of course—and he had the authority to give any part of it, or even all of it, to anyone who would submit to his authority. Let's confirm one very important fact. Adam was not the owner of the earth, sea and sky. He was simply the steward over Someone else's creation. Consequently, what was transferred to Satan through Adam's moral defeat was not ownership, but simply stewardship

what was transferred to Satan through Adam's moral defeat was not ownership, but simply stewardship management.

management. However, because of his insatiable ambition to be *"like the Most High"* (Isaiah 14;14), the devil assumed "ownership" of the earth and was willing to appoint himself managers who would be subservient to him.

Have you ever met someone who is not the owner of a piece of real estate, but was seeking to transact business with the said property as though it really belonged to him? It's like a tenant attempting to rent or even sell the apartment or house of his landlord. Unthinkable, isn't it? It is one thing to rent or sell a landlord's property to another, but it is outright madness to attempt to rent or, even worse, sell that property to the landlord, himself. Well, that's exactly what the devil attempted to do with Jesus in the wilderness of temptation. He told the Creator-Owner, "if you would only be subservient to me, I will give to you authority over the all the kingdoms of earth and the fame associated with them." It was a clear repeat of the old Eden lie with the hidden hook—*you will be like God, [but I will be the one controlling you]*, (Genesis 3:5, brackets mine). Thankfully, Jesus did not accept the devil's offer. Instead, He went on to defeat him and set the stage for humanity's complete deliverance from his dominion, and full restoration to a perfect union with God.

> *It is one thing to rent or sell a landlord's property to another, but it is outright madness to attempt to rent, even worse sell, that property to the landlord, himself.*

In the closing scenes of His life on earth, Jesus cited Satan as *the ruler of this world* in this triumphant declaration to His disciples: *I will no longer talk much with you, for the ruler of this world is coming, and he has nothing in Me"* (John 14:30). The ruler *of this world* is Christ's veiled reference to the temporary control Adam gave the evil one over the world. However, that control was limited in its scope because of the enmity[17] God had established against it. The prophetic Seed of the woman, Jesus Christ, stated unequivocally that Satan had NOTHING in Him. In other words, there was no element of the SELF-life virus—self-

---

[17]Genesis 3:15 – *"And I will put enmity between you and the woman, and between your seed and her Seed; He shall bruise your head, and you shall bruise His heel."*

preservation, self-empowerment, self-determination, and self-actualization[18]—in Him; for He did absolutely nothing that was self-driven or self-beneficial. The unswerving tenor of His life was, *"I can of Myself do nothing. As I hear, I judge; and My judgment is righteous, because I do not seek My own will but the will of the Father who sent Me"* (John 5:30). *"For I have come down from heaven, not to do My own will, but the will of Him who sent Me"* (John 6:38).

Understanding Our World

> *[15]Do not love the world or the things in the world. If anyone loves the world, the love of the Father is not in him. [16]For all that is in the world—<u>the lust of the flesh</u>, the <u>lust of the eyes</u>, and <u>the pride of life</u>—is not of the Father but is of the world. [17]And the world is passing away, and the lust of it; but he who does the will of God abides forever.*

1 John 2:15-17, emphasis mine

This scripture comes by way of an admonition not only for young people, but for all the inhabitants of the earth.[19] It would be natural for the immediate logical response to this caution to be: "Why? Why am I not to love the world? I live in it for God's sake!" "What's wrong with the world, anyway?" These responses are instinctive to SELF-life, and this is precisely the point about the hack

---

[18]American philosopher Abraham Maslow, who is credited for the theory of human motivation referred to as the Hierarchy of Human Needs, cites self-actualization (or the ideal self) as the ultimate goal of human aspiration—the overarching need for self-fulfillment through competence and control.
[19]See also Revelation 12:12, which also reveals Satan's hateful disposition towards the inhabitants of the earth.

our hacked "order of operation" has establish in us a default setting that gives priority to human intelligence over spirit-directed life...

of humanity. We have already been preconditioned to challenge anything that conflicts with our distorted sense of reality, because our hacked "order of operation" has established in us a default setting that gives priority to human intelligence over spirit-directed life—often referred to as intuition. This is the essence of human hacking, and the astute hacker of all times has designed a world system solely for the support of that very purpose—elevation of human thought over direction from what remains of God's spirit image in the soul.

Let's now examine our scripture more closely. It would appear that the world and its principles compete against the love of God in the heart of humanity, for the text says that if anyone loves the world, the love of God is not the ruling principle of his life. Further, we see that all that is in the world is not from the Father, our original Creator, but from some other

all that is in the world is driven by three lusting spirits that feed and cultivate the SELF-life virus in humanity...

entity—the devil.[20] From the text, we also see that all that is in the world is driven by three lusting spirits that feed and cultivate the SELF-life virus in humanity—namely, *the lust of the flesh* (physical cravings and their satisfaction), *the lust of the eyes* (coveting whatever the eyes see) and *the pride of life* (lust of self-glorification).

What is even most interesting is that the devil nurtured the very same lusts in Eve when he seduced her

---

[20]The Bible actually refers to the devil as *the god of this world (age)* in 2 Corinthians 4:3, 4.

to eat from the forbidden tree in Eden. The Bible says, *so when the woman saw that the tree was good for food* **[lust of the flesh]**, *that it was pleasant to the eyes* **[lust of the eyes]**, *and a tree desirable to make one wise* **[pride of life or lust of self-glorification]**, *she took of its fruit and ate. She also gave to her husband with her, and he ate* (Genesis 3:6, brackets mine). Quite amazing, isn't it? Well, there is more.

While in the wilderness of temptation, the evil one used the identical approach against Jesus. In his first attack, the devil, knowing that Jesus had fasted 40 days and was extremely hungry, enticed Him to satisfy His hunger by using His Spirit union with God to turn stones into bread (Luke 4:1-4). This was a direct appeal to the lust associated with self-preservation—*the lust of the flesh*— to induce Jesus to save Himself from hunger and possibly untimely death.

Next, the devil showed Jesus all the kingdoms of the world and offered Him "full" authority[21] over them if He would only worship before him—that is, acknowledge him as God and rightful owner (Luke 4:5-7). Through this temptation the evil one was seeking to engage the eyes of Jesus—*lust of the eyes*—to covet after worldly kingdom power and authority.

Finally, the shrewd tempter appealed to presumptuous human pride—*the pride of life or the lust of self-glorification*—in his attempt to get Jesus to obey his suggestion to throw Himself off the pinnacle of the city temple (Luke 4:9-11). In this last temptation, the devil challenged Jesus' claim to be the Son of God and dared Him to plunge off the heights of the temple since the Word of God said that God the Father will send His angels to catch

---

[21]This was the equivalent to the lie the devil told Eve in the Garden. *"You will be like God [but I will be God over you],"* (Genesis 3:5, brackets mine).

Him from falling to His death.[22]

Clearly, the principles of operation in the world are fundamentally at odds with the God of creation. The underlying change of humanity's default setting predisposes the race to rely predominantly on intellectual reasoning, while, at the same time, downgrading reality to only what could be perceived by the natural senses. The broken union with God brought spiritual and intellectual darkness (Ephesians 4:18), loss of true identity and a distorted sense of reality. Leaning on this masked ignorance,[23] Satan continuously uses his three lusting spirits—**the lust of the flesh, the lust of the eyes**, and **the lust of self-glorification**—to manipulate and control all human thought and behavior.

The evil one has made it virtually impossible for any natural person to conceive of a life outside the philosophical and social norms of this world. Such an outlook goes against the grain of everyday human living. That is why choosing to be a devoted follower of Jesus Christ is such a difficult decision for the average individual. Living from the world perspective and living for Christ are based on two fundamentally opposing realities that will always be at odds with each other. One is self-centered, the other is God-centered. One is driven by the spirit of fear and lust, the other by the spirit of faith and love. In his first epistle, the apostle John expressed this basic difference in this way:

> *The evil one has made it virtually impossible for any natural person to conceive of a life outside the philosophical and social norms of this world.*

---

[22]SEE Psalm 91:11, 12.

[23]The ignorance is masked because it is passed off as worldly wisdom and intellectualism. SEE also James 3:14-16. More will be said about this in the next chapter.

4"You are of God, little children, and have overcome them, because He who is in you is greater than he who is in the world. 5They are of the world. Therefore, they speak as of the world, and the world hears them. 6We are of God. He who knows God hears us; he who is not of God does not hear us. By this we know <u>the spirit of truth</u> and <u>the spirit of error</u>."

1 John 4:4-6, emphasis mine

Jesus also cautioned His disciples about the world that would be strikingly at odds with them:

18"If the world hates you, you know that it hated Me before it hated you. 19If you were of the world the world would love its own. Yet because you are not of the world, but I chose you out of the world, therefore the world hates you."

John 15:18, 19

How many of those who profess to be disciples really believe that they are not of this world? Unless a person is brought into a clear revelation about the true nature of this world, it would be relatively easy for him to be woefully deceived concerning the reality of his life in this world. Without some measure

How we view the world will influence how we live and express our lives in it.

of divine intervention, the hack of humanity has made it near impossible for anyone to win over the treacherous plays and counter-plays of life in this world. How we view the world will influence how we live and express our lives in it.

The Viral Server

³And even if our gospel is veiled [hidden, misunderstood], it is veiled [hidden, misunderstood], to those who are perishing, ⁴in whose case <u>the god of this world</u> [Satan] <u>has blinded the minds of the unbelieving</u> so that they might not see the light of the gospel of the glory of Christ, who is the image of God.

2 Corinthians 4:3, 4, NASB, brackets and emphasis mine

The Bible records Christ's complete victory over the devil and his kingdom of darkness in the following terms: *Having disarmed principalities and powers, He made a public spectacle of them, triumphing over them in it* (Colossians 2:15). When the Savior cried, *"It is finished"* on the cross of Calvary, the power and finality of this exclamation reverberated throughout the universe and shook the foundation of Satan's kingdom. It marked the fulfillment of the prophetic crushing of the serpent's head (Genesis 3:15), and forever sealed the fate of the devil and his demonic cohort. Through this authoritative public display of His victory on the cross and His glorious resurrection from the dead shortly thereafter, Christ rendered powerless all the demonic arsenals of Satan. The salvation of humanity was forever secured.

However, although God made adequate provision in Christ for the redemption of humanity from demonic hacking, the good news (Gospel) of this gracious act had to be made known to a fallen, disillusioned world. Nevertheless, it was, and still is, an integral part of Satan's agenda to obscure God's message of hope from His oppressed children. The above scripture tells us that *the god of this world*—Satan—mounted a campaign of *interception, distraction, misrepresentation* and *confusion* in his effort to blind the minds of earth's inhabitants from receiving a clear revelation of what God has made available for them through Jesus Christ.

Just as a skillful computer programmer sets up a server to run a Mac or PC network, so the devil has redesigned our world to function as a viral sever to enhance the operation of his SELF-life virus in humanity. We have already seen how Satan used his control over our world to try to seduce Jesus to sin against His Father. In his second temptation,[24] he told Jesus that he could give the world and its glory to whomever he wishes, if only the receiver would serve him. This is enough to make a person pause, or even shudder at the possibility of being an active operative of Satan on the earth.

Shockingly, the Bible tells us quite forthrightly that *the whole world lies under the sway [power] of the evil one* (1 John 5:19). This text is a heart-stopper and begs the question, "Does that includes me?" I am afraid all of humanity has been infected by the evil germ of fallen Adam.[25] Clearly, the devil has more control over this world than humanity has accredited to him, and he is using it as a tool to facilitate and manipulate the thought-life and behavior of the race. The Bible makes reference to this in Paul's letter to the Christian believers who once lived in the ancient city of Ephesus.

¹And you He made alive, who were dead in

---

[24] ... *"⁶All this authority I will give You, and their glory; for this has been delivered to me, and **I give it to whomever I wish**. ⁷Therefore, if You will worship before me, all will be Yours"* - Luke 4:6, 7.
[25] *Therefore, just as sin came into the world through one man [Adam], and death came through sin, and so death spread to all because all have sinned* – Romans 5:12, NRSV, brackets mine.

*trespasses and sins, [2]in which you once walked according to <u>the course of this world</u>, according to the <u>prince of the power of the air, the spirit</u> <u>who now works in the sons of disobedience</u>, [3]among whom also we all once conducted ourselves in <u>the lusts of our flesh, fulfilling the desires of the flesh and of the mind</u>, and were **by nature children of wrath**, just as the others.*

Ephesians 2:1-3

The apostle was explaining to the Ephesian believers that before they experienced God's salvation in Jesus Christ, not only were they spiritually dead, but that their entire life's outlook and actions were driven or dictated by *the course of this world*—worldly philosophies, principles and ideas, or Satan's viral server. Moreover, he further clarified that *the prince of the power of the air* (the devil) was the mastermind behind the world server, and that he was using it to nurture his rebellious spirit (the SELF-life virus) in humanity—*the sons [children] of disobedience*. It is this viral server of worldliness that feeds the greedy, immoral, lusting spirits that eat at the souls of humankind.[26] What is most alarming in the apostle's description is the fact that the devil has transferred his evil, hateful nature to humanity, driving people to commit unimaginable acts against God, the creation, and one another.

Sadly, today we have grown accustom to the wickedness and cruelties of this age. Ponder for a moment the heavy weight of the awful conditions that have become a new normal for the human race. Humankind,

---

[26]See Ephesians 4:17-19.

the devil has more control over this world than humanity has accredited to him, and he is using it as a tool to facilitate and manipulate the thought-life and behavior of the race.

created in the image of God to be the expression of His righteous nature, was infiltrated by Satan who masterfully distorted that image. Now he incites humanity to express the hostilities of his wrathful nature. Consequently, instead of being children of love in union with the Father of love, humanity has become children of wrath in union with the father of wrath[27] —Satan.

The Rise of Humanism

The Holy Scriptures tell us that *God hath made man [mankind] upright; but they have sought out many inventions* (Ecclesiastes 7:29, KJV, brackets mine). One of the greatest results from the lie spun by the evil one in the Garden of Eden— *"...you will be like God..."* —was the rise of a philosophical outlook of life called humanism[28] during the 14th century. This view of life places the individual at the center (really, as god) of his own universe, and emphasizes human rationalism as the only means of human problem solving and need satisfaction. The push of progressive humanism is to evict God from the public discourse and allow that space to be ruled solely by human reason, with the intent to re-shape the thought-life and behaviors of the masses.

At the root of this philosophy is the worship of the

---

[27]Revelation 12:12 speaks to the devil's wrathful entry into our world.
[28]See *https://americanhumanist.org/what-is-humanism/definition-of-humanism/*.
Humanism is a progressive philosophy of life that, without theism or other supernatural beliefs, affirms our ability and responsibility to lead ethical lives of personal fulfillment that aspire to the greater good.

SELF[29], driven and facilitated by self-preservation, self-empowerment, self-determination and self-actualization. No question, Satan has used humanism as a captivating vehicle to mask his presence in, and strengthen his grip on, the human soul. Consequently, the evil one expresses himself through the

The push of progressive humanism is to evict God from the public discourse and allow that space to be ruled solely by human reason...

ideology of the humanist saying, "I am my own god, and I could do good or evil all by myself." As a matter of fact, the positioning strategy of the American Humanist Association says, "Good Without God."[30] The subtle deception of the human SELF is the belief that it is inherently good; but the sad reality is that the very ones who believe they are inherently good are often surprised by the evil of their own making. Little do such individuals know that the unsuspecting mixture of good and evil is the poisonous fruit from the tree[31] of Satan's evil nature.

While on a recent visit to a Caribbean island where I served as a pastor many years ago, I came across a couple who had no room in their lives for God. The wife proudly said to me, "I am my own god. I decide what's good or bad, right or wrong for me." I calmly replied, "If I should live by your truth, then my god is pretty small don't you think? Tell me, what do you do when you come to situations in your life that are much bigger than your little SELF-god?" She said, "I see your point, and I have had, and still have, many such

---

[29]The worship of the SELF is really the worship of Satan who reigns as "God" in the human soul.

[30]Ibid., 13.

[31] *16And the Lord God commanded the man, saying, "Of every tree of the garden you may freely eat; 17but of **the tree of the knowledge of good and evil** you shall not eat, for in the day that you eat of it you shall surely die."* – Genesis 2:16, 17

moments. I guess there is nothing that I could do about those, can I?" Quite simply, I replied, "You already have the answer to that question."

It is nothing short of amazing to see the dramatic rise of self-centeredness and selfishness in our world today.

Satan has used humanism as a captivating vehicle to mask his presence and strengthen his grip on the human soul.

Moreover, the increasing number of social media outlets only creates gateways for the unabashed expression and display of the shallowness of the human soul. The compelling virus of the lusting spirits[32] in humanity generates a ceaseless yearning for recognition and acceptance of the SELF that has suppressed moral restraint and social responsibility among the confused masses. As the center of its own universe, SELF becomes a law unto itself and does what is right in its own eyes, according to its own "wisdom." However, the truth is that SELF with all its so-called wisdom is much too small to handle all the intolerable stresses and growing complexities associated with everyday human existence.

God and the Humanistic Worldview

For as much as humanism marginalizes God, and, in some cases, disavows Him altogether, divine inspiration pushes back against the wisdom of this humanistic age. Here is God's attitude towards the wisdom of this viral world server:

[20]Where is the wise person? Where is the teacher

---

[32]*The lust of the flesh* or physical cravings; *the lust of the eyes* or envy and greed; and *the pride of life* or the lust of self-glorification.

124

of the law? Where is the philosopher of this age? Has not God made foolish the wisdom of the world? [21]For since in the wisdom of God the world through its wisdom did not know him, God was pleased through the foolishness of what was preached to save those who believe.

1 Corinthians 1:20, 21, NIV, emphasis mine

And again,

[13]Who is wise and understanding among you? Let him show by good conduct that his works are done in the meekness of wisdom. [14]But if you have bitter envy and self-seeking in your hearts, do not boast and lie against the truth. [15]This wisdom does not descend from above, but is earthly, sensual, demonic. [16]For where envy and self-seeking exist, confusion and every evil thing are there. [17]But the wisdom that is from above is first pure, then peaceable, gentle, willing to yield, full of mercy and good fruits, without partiality and without hypocrisy.

James 3:13-17, emphasis mine

Besides challenging the scholars and philosophers who seek to shape the intellectual, political and social discourses of this world, the above scriptures state very clearly that there is a wisdom that comes from God above and another that comes from the pit of hell. The evil one uses this earthly wisdom to influence and control unwary souls in the world. The scriptures also reveal that God has set Himself against the wisdom of this world not only because He knows its operating source, but also because that wisdom promotes envy, self-seeking, sensuality, confusion and all types of evil in this world. Such wisdom reflects only the expressions of captured, carnal souls that often vaunts themselves against God's will and authority. Therefore, the Bible says that God not only calls such wisdom foolish and futile, but He also allows the so-called wise people of this world to fall victims to their own crafty schemes.

> [18]Let no one deceive himself. If anyone among you seems to be wise in this age, let him become a fool that he may become wise. [19]For <u>the wisdom of this world is foolishness with God</u>. For it is written, "<u>He catches the wise in their own craftiness</u>"; [20]and again, "The Lord knows the thoughts of the wise, that <u>they are futile</u>."

> 1 Corinthians 3:18-20, emphasis mine

Moreover, Christ, Himself, said that God hides His revelations from those who consider themselves wise and intelligent according to this world's standard, and delights to reveal Himself to those of a humble, teachable disposition.[33] As a matter of fact, the prophet Isaiah describes God as the One *Who frustrates the signs of the babblers [pundits or commentators], And drives diviners [fortune-tellers or forecasters] mad; Who turns wise men*

The evil one uses this earthly wisdom to influence and control unwary souls in the world.

---

[33]Matthew 11:25, 26.

backward, and makes their knowledge foolishness (Isaiah 44:24, 25, brackets mine).

The World is Passing Away

Since demonic forces drive the wisdom of this world, and the evil one uses this wisdom as a gigantic, network server to facilitate his deadly, SELF-life virus in humanity, the Bible gives repeated admonition regarding the danger of allowing worldly philosophies, principles and ideas to shape our life outlook and behavior. The apostle Paul cautions us through his letter to the Christians in ancient Colossae,

> *"Don't let anyone capture you with empty philosophies and high-sounding nonsense that come from human thinking [humanism] and from the spiritual powers [demonic forces] of this world, rather than from Christ."*

> Colossians 2:8, NLT[34] , brackets mine

The prophet Isaiah also declares,

> [6]*Seek the Lord while He may be found, call upon Him while He is near. [7]Let the wicked forsake his way, And the unrighteous man his thoughts; Let him return to the Lord, And He will have mercy on him; And to our God, For He will abundantly pardon. [8]"For My thoughts are not your thoughts, nor are your ways My ways," says the Lord. [9]"For as the heavens are higher*

---

[34]New Living Translation of the Holy Bible.

than the earth, so are My ways higher than your ways, And My thoughts than your thoughts.

Isaiah 55:6-9

While the world, through humanism, exalts the wisdom and reason of humankind, it reels under the abuses exacted upon it by those who proclaim themselves the brightest and wisest among us. Indeed, intellectuals believe that their perception of reality and the ways they think about it are right, but they cannot override or hinder the thoughts and purposes of God.[35] Therefore, the counsel of Isaiah is very pertinent for dealing with the present stressful conditions of our world, and speaks to the conversation of this book. If humanity fails to trust the supreme knowledge and wisdom of God, it will be impossible for the race to deliver itself from the misery and pain resulting from satanic hacking. However, this is the exact purpose of the devil's plot of against the race. He seeks persistently to promote human distrust in the Creator, while at the same time promoting absolute confidence in SELF-life.[36] Additionally, he uses all the demonic elements of the world to facilitate this very objective. Nevertheless, the Bible warns,

> *If humanity fails to trust ...God, it will be impossible for the race to deliver itself from the misery and pain resulting from satanic hacking.*

[15]Do not love the world or the things in the world. If anyone loves the world, the love of the Father is not in him. [16]For all that is in the world—

---

[35]See Isaiah 46:8-11.
[36]SELF-life is really Lucifer's evil spirit reigning like "God" in the human soul. See also Isaiah 14:12-14.

*the lust of the flesh, the lust of the eyes, and the pride of life—**is not of the Father** but is of the world. [17]And **the world is passing away**, and the lust of it; but he who does the will of God abides forever.*

1 John 2:15-17, emphasis mine

Everything in the world that appeals to the viral spirit of lust in humanity is passing away, and therefore, to that extent everything in the world is not real or lasting. The devastating effects of the global pandemic brought about by the Covid-19 viral outbreak is an unmistakable, stark reminder of this fact. Almost overnight, all the major human systems that hold our world together seemed to collapse before our very eyes, revealing that absolutely nothing in this world has built-in sustainability. Everything goes through the cycle of the curse called death and eventually passes away. It is strangely incredible and heartbreaking that just when a person thinks he has arrived at his lifelong goal or dream, that his life is cut short, that the goalpost he set has shifted unexpectedly, and that what was once a dream morphed into a terrible nightmare. Life suddenly appears terribly unfair and the human mind seeks someone to blame for its grave misfortune. By default, through Satan's hack, people are moved to pin that blame on God,[37] just as the evil one would have them to do.

Sadly, the devil is still trading the pleasures and glories of this world for lordship over the souls of people, just as he attempted to do with Jesus in the wilderness. He continues to use the world as a large-scale viral server to

---

[37]See Genesis 3:11-13. Adam and Eve blamed God for their misfortune caused by their own disobedience to His command.

support the spirit of his life in humanity. We have already seen that the whole world lies under the powerful influence of the evil one (1 John 5:19), and by yielding to his lust-gratifying schemes and propositions, many voluntarily place themselves under his rulership. However, the grave warning of Jesus still stands as a guardrail against Satan's viral deceptions: *"For what shall it profit a man, if he shall gain the whole world, and lose his own soul? Or what shall a man give in exchange for his soul"* (Mark 8:36, 37, KJV)?

In this regard, Paul's counsel proves quite necessary for all God's children: *Don't copy the behavior and customs of this world, but let God transform you into a new person by changing the way you think. Then you will learn to know God's will for you, which is good and pleasing and perfect* (Romans 12:2, NLT). It is my hope and prayer that this book will assist in making the implementation of this counsel an informed and successful experience.

[14]For we know that the law is spiritual, but I am carnal, sold under sin. [15]For what I am doing, I do not understand. For what I will to do, that I do not practice; but what I hate, that I do. [16]If, then, I do what I will not to do, I agree with the law that it is good. [17]But now, it is no longer I who do it, but sin that dwells in me. [18]For I know that in me (that is, in my flesh) nothing good dwells; for to will is present with me, but how to perform what is good I do not find. [19]For the good that I will to do, I do not do; but the evil I will not to do, that I practice. [20]Now if I do what I will not to do, it is no longer I who do it, but sin that dwells in me. [21]I find then a law, that evil is present with me, the one who wills to do good. [22]For I delight in the law of God according to the inward man. [23]But I see another law in my members, warring against the law of my mind, and bringing me into captivity to the law of sin which is in my members.

Roman 7:14-23

9

The Hack and Identity Corruption

What we have examined so far is a basic summary of Satan's plot against humanity—what that plot really is, how it was initiated, what it has accomplished and how it is maintained as an ongoing threat against basic human existence. Before we turn our attention to God's answer to this hack of humanity, I believe it is critically important for us to take a candid look at how this demonic operation is manifested in everyday life. Without this understanding, individuals will not feel the need to change the course of their thinking and behavior and may continue to be unsuspecting victims of the oppressive tactics of the evil one.

Interestingly, whenever a computer is hacked, the owner soon recognizes the misdeed, but the computer itself has absolutely no knowledge that its internal operational system has been infiltrated and altered. It simply carries out the alternative commands that the hacker implanted in its "order of operation." In a similar sense, humanity has been hacked but does not know that its original operating system has been radically altered and reprogrammed to function contrary to its created order. As a matter of fact, most people think that their current operating system is an endowment from God—that they are "created" in His image[1] with the power of reason to be independent masters of their own lives. No thinking of this order is further from the truth.

Although we may not be willing to acknowledge that we have been victimized by the demonic mastermind, we do not have to look very far to see all the abuses that human wisdom and self-centeredness have heaped upon itself and our world. Like a hacked computer, humanity is simply carrying out the corrupt commands of a pernicious operating order, implanted with the SELF-life virus by Satan, the master hacker. The working of human intelligence has superseded and dominated the influence of the Creator's bastion of truth and uprightness initially formed in humankind before the tragic fall of the race. Logic and common sense, driven by self-preserving fear, often secure easy victory over the voice of conscience when we are confronted by critical choices that test our strength of character. Ultimately, the identifying mark of satanic hacking is the subservience of the fallen human spirit to the deity of human intelligence.

While we may not be able to explore all the avenues through which Satan's hack of humanity is exhibited, we will cover some major arenas in which this plot is clearly displayed. In reading through and arriving at this chapter of the book, I believe the Holy Spirit has been your Helper as He is mine, in guiding your understanding of these truths so that you might experience the greatest joy of your life. As you continue with me in digging a little deeper in this topic, I

Ultimately, the identifying mark of satanic hacking is the subservience of the fallen human spirit to the deity of human intelligence.

---

[1]Genesis 5:1-5 – Only Adam and Eve were created in the image of God. All other human beings were born or begotten—not created—in the marred image of fallen Adam.

do wish to caution you that the Holy Spirit's revelation of these truths may evoke some unwelcome emotions in you. Such exposure may produce a sense of guilt, condemnation and fear as was displayed by Adam and Eve after their disgraceful fall.[2] You may be tempted to close this book and walk away. **Please don't**.

The word of God is like a large mirror that reveals the broken reality of the human condition. Aversion to the truth of this reality tends to summon the hacking effect of self-preservation and all the negative thoughts and feelings associated with it. Also, past encounters with uninformed, religious zealots may have provoked you to distance yourself from anything and anyone associated with religion, and, in many instances, from God and His word. God inspired me to write this book to bring hope and assurance to hacked humanity, including religious zealots and those whom they judge. God is not against humanity, but for humanity; not against sinners, but for sinners. This must be clearly understood. Humanity and sinners are one and the same— identical victims of the devil's devious hacking. The Bible declares quite plainly that *"There is none righteousness, no, not one... for All have sinned and fall short of the glory of God"* (Romans 3:10, 23).

Let me take a moment to confirm some undeniable truths about God in the Scriptures before we get into the meat of this chapter.

> *[16]For God so <u>loved the world</u> that He gave His only begotten Son, that <u>whoever believes in Him</u> should not perish but have everlasting life. [17]For <u>God did not send His Son into the world to</u>*

---

[2]Genesis 3:8-10.

condemn the world, but that the world through Him might be saved.
John 3:16, 17, emphasis mine

8But God demonstrates His own love toward us, in that while we were still sinners, Christ died for us.
Romans 5:8, emphasis mine

32I have come to call not those who think they are righteous, but those who know they are sinners and need to repent.
Luke 5:32, NLT, emphasis mine

19...God was in Christ, reconciling the world to Himself, no longer counting people's sins against them. And he gave us this wonderful message of reconciliation [not condemnation or alienation].

2 Corinthians 5:19, NLT, brackets and emphasis mine

All of the above scriptures confirm why the Gospel is called the "good news" of salvation and not the bad news of condemnation that many religionists proclaim. Far too many are still pushing the negative, fear-based message of alienation and condemnation instead of the positive, faith-inspiring message of reconciliation and justification— acquittal of all sins—through faith in Jesus Christ. It is very encouraging to know that from God's standpoint, the whole

God is not against humanity, but for humanity; not against sinners, but for sinners.

world of sinners is already reconciled to Him through the death of His Son, Jesus Christ. This is the highest note[3] of the Gospel, and all believers must learn how to sing it.

However, I must hasten to say that reconciliation (making peace) and justification (complete acquittal of sins) are not one and the same thing. God made the first move in reconciling all His hacked children to Himself by the ransom He paid for their sins through the death of His Son. Now all sinners have the option of completing the transaction of acquittal (called justification) by accepting God's payment of death for their sins through the crucifixion of Jesus Christ. Should sinners refuse to accept God's payment for all their sins through the death of His Son—Jesus Christ, then they themselves will bear the penalty of God's eternal judgment of their sins. Consequently, the sinner's fate is in his own hands, and God's window of mercy—the very short time we have on earth—is his opportunity to make the greatest choice of his very brief life. I will explain this more fully in the last chapter.

Identity Corruption

Now that I have given you a little heads up on what's coming, let us get on to the real business of this chapter. When God created Adam, his identity was clearly defined by God's spirit-image within him. Adam had absolutely no identity apart from the life of God, through his unbroken communion with his Maker. However, when Satan succeeded in breaching this spirit union, he replaced the image of God in the soul by the image of the human SELF, giving

---

[3]*This is a trustworthy saying, and everyone should accept it:* ***"Christ Jesus came into the world to save sinners"****—and I am the worst of them all* (1 Timothy 1:15, NLT, emphasis mine).

preeminence to SELF-life and human intelligence over divine spirit. Through this self-centered virus, the evil one has been able to challenge God's preeminence and authority in the human soul and change the truth about God and human existence into a lie.

Many have argued that God has given them a brain so they can think and figure out life's demands for themselves. I used to be one of those. Such thinking is void of the understanding that God shared His Spirit-image with humanity so that His children could think and act like Him, not contrary to Him. However, something catastrophic disrupted this divine order in humanity when the father of our race, Adam, broke ties with his Creator. The apostle Paul gives us a very vivid picture of this dreadful tragedy that brings confirmation to the theme of this book.

When God created Adam, his identity was clearly defined by God's spirit-image within him.

> [20]*For ever since the world was created, people have seen the earth and sky. Through everything God made, they can clearly see His invisible qualities—His eternal power and divine nature. So <u>they have no excuse for not knowing God</u>.* [21]<u>*Yes, they knew God, but they wouldn't worship Him as God or even give Him thanks*</u>. *And they began to think up foolish ideas of what God was like. As a result, their minds became dark and confused.* [22]<u>*Claiming to be wise, they instead became utter fools*</u>. [23]*And instead of worshiping the glorious, ever-living God, they worshiped idols made to look like mere people and birds and animals and reptiles.*

THE HACK AND IDENTITY CORRUPTION

*24So God abandoned them to do whatever shameful things their hearts desired. As a result, they did vile and degrading things with each other's bodies. 25**They traded the truth about God for a lie**. So they worshiped and served the things God created instead of the Creator Himself, who is worthy of eternal praise! Amen.*

26That is why God abandoned them to their shameful desires. Even the women turned against the natural way to have sex and instead indulged in sex with each other. 27And the men, instead of having normal sexual relations with women, burned with lust for each other. Men did shameful things with other men, and as a result of this sin, they suffered within themselves the penalty they deserved.

28Since they thought it foolish to acknowledge God, He abandoned them to their foolish thinking and let them do things that should never be done. 29Their lives became full of every kind of wickedness, sin, greed, hate, envy, murder, quarreling, deception, malicious behavior, and gossip. 30They are backstabbers, haters of God, insolent, proud, and boastful. They invent new ways of sinning, and they disobey their parents. 31They refuse to understand, break their promises, are heartless, and have no mercy. 32They know God's justice requires that those who do these things deserve to die, yet they do them anyway. Worse yet, they encourage others to do them, too.

Romans 1:20-32, NLT, emphasis mine

Please do not miss God's point in the above scriptures. It is not to condemn humanity, but to hold up a mirror to sensitize the race regarding its depravity and its true condition before the Creator. Moreover, this uncompromising review is given to highlight humanity's desperate need of redemption from total self-destruction. Sadly, many religionists have used these scriptures to pronounce judgement upon beleaguered people who are anxiously trying to find themselves and their way in the agitated whirlpool of human chaos. However, such behavior does not harmonize with the proper use of the Scriptures. The Bible itself tells us not only how it should be used and applied to the life of a person, but also what God's purpose was in giving it to us. It declares, *"All Scripture is given by inspiration of God, and is profitable for doctrine, for reproof, for correction, for instruction in righteousness, [17]that the man of God may be complete, thoroughly equipped for every good work"* (2 Timothy 3:15, 16, emphasis mine).

Nowhere does it say in the text that the Scriptures were given to judge or condemn a person. The closest approach to that position from the text is the word "reproof". This word is translated from the original New Testament Greek *elegchos*, which gives the idea of conviction, or bringing about an awareness of wrong thought or behavior in a person. However, what is most profound about the above text is the end goal of the all Scripture—that the child of God may be a complete or mature and wholesome person, morally equipped for every good work. So, God's goal is not condemnation, but elevation of every person who is willing to interact with and live by the Holy Scriptures. Particularly, I like the rendering of the New Living Translation of 2 Timothy 3:16, 17, which reads, *"All Scripture is inspired by God and is useful to teach us what is true and to make us realize what is wrong in our lives. It corrects us when we are wrong and teaches us to do what is right. [17]God uses it to prepare and equip his people to do every good work.* This is not just hopeful; it is quite refreshing.

While the Bible outlines the repulsive sins and practices of hacked humanity, it is also very forceful in its warning against self-righteous people who think it is their prerogative to pronounce judgement on the misdeeds and mishaps of others. Please notice how the Scriptures address this issue immediately following its portrayal of the depravity of the human race in Romans 1:20-32.

> *[1]You, therefore, have no excuse, you who pass judgment on someone else, for at whatever point you judge another, you are condemning yourself, because you who pass judgment do the same things. [2]Now we know that God's judgment against those who do such things is based on truth. [3]So when you, a mere human being, pass judgment on them and yet do the same things, do you think you will escape God's judgment? [4]Or do you show contempt for the riches of his kindness, forbearance and patience, not realizing that God's kindness is intended to lead you to repentance?*
>
> Romans 2:1-4, NIV

Through his hack of humanity, Satan incites people to disavow, disrespect and dishonor the God of creation, and to follow the wicked imaginations of their depraved spirit and mind. Our biblical text (Romans 1:24-27 above) says that God allowed the ugly virus of self-centeredness to display itself quite openly so humanity could experience the abhorrent results of choosing a life void of His authority and influence. Although these scriptures were written many centuries ago, they still aptly describe the moral decadence of humanity that is so openly visible today.

It is quite appalling and somewhat unbelievable to see how the progressive decline in moral clarity has left so many people bereft of shame and confused about their identity. The legitimate identity of humanity was established at creation, embedded in God's spirit image that was breathed into Adam's lifeless body. Once that image was disconnected from its Source, humanity was at the mercy of the evil one. Satan was determined to change EVERY truth of God into a lie in order to advance his hateful, destructive agenda against heaven and earth.

Today, the peoples and governments of our world are on edge because of the growing impact of the expanding pluralist expression of the human SELF. The viral effect of the satanic hack on the foundation of human identity is clearly reflected in the rising perplexities with regards to the current conversations about gender categorization, recognition and expression in our world. As the list of gender classification continues to increase[4], so too does the confusion and stress levels among the people caught in its rapidly changing current. Young and old are yearning for

---

[4]https://abcnews.go.com/blogs/headlines/2014/02/heres-a-list-of-58-gender-options-for-facebook-users. ABC News identified at least 58 gender options that Facebook made available to it users.

recognition and the free expression of their identity as they strive for their place and space into the already burdened, bewildered, anxious societies of our world. Needless to say, this appears to be the brewing of a perfect storm for chaotic confrontations and massive relational conflicts, the reality of which no earthly system can manage or contain.

Race[5] Relations

The issue of gender classification and free expression is only the tip of the identity corruption iceberg. Much, much more lies beneath. The loss of its authentic identity in God put humanity at risk against many other deceptive evils in the devil's arsenal. Chief among them is the matter of race relations. Many who are caught up in racial rivalries are not fully aware of the real underlying forces that drive the tribal tensions and tumults that have their engagement. Tribalism is as old as the fall of humanity and is a reflection of the combined effects of three heartbreaking factors that resulted from this tragic event—namely, the loss of true identity, the distortion of reality and the viral driver of self-preservation.

Although I have already dealt with these three elements in previous chapters, it is necessary for me to show how they have a direct impact on the issue of race relations in this section. Human identity and the concept of reality are directly related to one another. God created humankind in His own image so that humanity would be

---

[5] https://en.wikipedia.org/wiki/Race_(human_categorization).
A race is a grouping of humans based on shared physical or social qualities into categories generally viewed as distinct by society. The term was first used to refer to speakers of a common language and then to denote national affiliations. By the 17th century the term began to refer to physical traits.

a true expression of Himself. Apart from his spirit-image union with God, Adam had absolutely no other authentic way of identifying himself. Moreover, Adam's understanding of reality grew out of his understanding of himself through his relationship with God who created him. To him, reality was God and the perfect expression of God's image in him as it interacted with everything created in time and space.

However, when Adam decided to obey the voice of his wife instead of the directive of God that was crying out from his spirit's conscience, he severed ties not only from the Source of his true identity, but also from the Foundation of his view of reality.[6] From that moment forward, Adam and Eve defined themselves by the nakedness of their outward

> To him [Adam], reality was God, and the perfect expression of God's image in him as it interacted with everything created in time and space.

appearance instead of by the inward reality of God's spirit-image. Consequently, humanity's rebellion against God led to identity confusion, reality inversion,[7] self-centeredness and fear, and these pernicious elements gave rise to race consciousness and racial perversions.

Race is purely a physical experience of the world defined by physical genetic elements like blood, eyes, hair, skin, nose, etc. Once a person's identity and sense of reality are defined by his race, it is quite easy for that person to see himself as different from another human being of another

---

[6]Review Chapter 7 for more details about this.

[7]Reality inversion means turning God's concept of reality inside out, limiting it only to what could be perceived by the human senses, while, at the same time, discounting or denying the spiritual or invisible elements of God's creation. Reality begins and ends with the invisible God who created things visible and invisible and brought forth the visible out of the invisible. SEE also Colossians 1:16; Hebrews 11:3

race and gravitate to those of his own kind. Moreover, when this distorted sense of reality is combined with the overpowering, viral driver of self-preservation and the distorted perception of the scarcity of resources, it becomes the perfect environment for nurturing a culture of survival of the fittest and richest. Self-preservation promotes fear, and fear drives greed and every evil thing known to humankind.

At the heart of ALL forms of racism is inherent identity corruption and confusion...

However, race is not the reality of who a person genuinely is before God. Samuel, the prophet, would remind us that *the Lord does not see as man [humanity] sees; for man [humanity] looks at the outward appearance, but the Lord looks at the heart [the spirit driving the person]* (1 Samuel 16:7, brackets mine). In other words, God's identification of a person is determined by the condition of His image in that person, and not the individual's physical appearance. Poor racial relations are based on purely physical and psychological grounds, never on authentic spiritual grounds, even though some may dare to think so.

The spirit-image of God in humanity has absolutely no racial identity or identifiers like physical traits or features. Whenever that image governs human interaction and conversation racial tension and tribalism are diminished significantly. Nevertheless, the sad reality is that because of the fall, human intelligence often overrides God's directives in the depraved human spirit-image. Moreover, when human reason is driven by the convergence of identity confusion, fear, and a twisted sense of reality, the unavoidable result is racial tension, racial inequalities and all types of conflicts.

At the heart of all manifestations of racism is inherent identity corruption and confusion—a severe disconnection from what remains of God's image in humanity. Yet the greater evil is the unfounded fear that this confusion generates through reality distortion, self-preservation and the domination of misguided human reason. The imprudent tribal instinct evoked by the veiled perception of the scarcity of life's resources and the survival pressure of self-protecting fear, often drive otherwise seemingly decent people to shocking, inhumane behavior. All these elements are the by-products of the satanic hack of the ONE race called human.

Consequently, the global pursuit for racial equality, with all its noteworthy humanitarian ideals, is an elusive myth based upon the false assumption of racial identity. The inherent flaw of this identity is that it emphasizes the unique physical and social differences of people groups than the fundamental element of all human existence—the breath of life and image of God that all humanity shares in common. This misconception is a result of the satanic hack that changed Adam's concept of reality, making his physical perception more real and dominant that his disconnected, inward, spirit image.

The spirit-image of God in humanity has absolutely no race identity or identifier.

It is this core character flaw, which promotes reality distortion, the evil one uses to fuel racial conflict by the subtle distraction of an array of things that appeal to the physical appearance and racial sustainability. Accordingly, the underlying driver of racial intolerance is strife over who will have control over the accumulation and distribution of the resources that contribute to the life, liberty and the pursuit of happiness among the races.

In most recent time, the world stood horrified as it witnessed a white, law-enforcement officer, unlawfully murdered an already subdued black man by pressing his knee into his neck until the last breath left the victim's body. This unspeakable, senseless incident ignited swift responses of protests in the United States of America, where the criminal act occurred, and all over the world—the like of which has never been seen. It is so very ironic that the very nation that proudly boast *"We hold these truths to be self-evident, that all men are created equal, that they are endowed by their Creator with certain unalienable Rights, that among these are Life, Liberty and the pursuit of Happiness,"*[8] has a bloody, checkered history of racial injustice and abuse of the African American and other minority races.

However, this is not at all surprising, for wherever identity corruption and confusion exists, racial injustice and all other forms of human indignities will continue to occur. Once the image of God in humanity is no longer the ruling disposition of the soul, any type of evil, coldhearted behavior will thrive and multiply. As long as human reason trumps God's spirit in the soul, selfishness with its accompanying evils will govern all human existence. Satan's hack of humanity is exceedingly real, and the fallen race, on its own, does not possess the capacity or ability to rebuff or refute the insidious, demonic attacks from an enemy within itself. Evil has a way of showing up unexpectedly in odd places and we are often left in troubling wonder and great consternation.

> *As long as human reason trumps God's spirit in the soul, selfishness with its accompanying evils will govern all human existence.*

[8]Excerpt from The Declaration of Independence, July 4, 1776.

The Religious World

It is not very surprising to discover the footprint of identity confusion in the world of religion. Nowhere is this disturbing crisis more evident than in this area of human existence. Adam's separation from the Creator and His Life produced a yearning emptiness in the soul of humanity that could only be filled by the resident presence of God Himself in the human spirit. Moreover, this emptiness also created a deep, abiding fear that propelled humanity on a perpetual search for someone or something bigger than itself as a grounding for its sense of need for safety, provision, lasting peace, joy and fulfillment. This search, active or passive, is often manifested in many forms of human expression, ranging from the worship and service of God or some other form of deity, to the relentless chasing after all kinds of pleasure. All of this floundering represents humanity's futile effort to fill the bottomless abyss of the human SELF. The baneful result is the growing kaleidoscope of religions, faddism and other cultic movements we see in our world. According to Adherents.com,[9] there are over 44,000 adherent statistical citations for more than 4,300 different faith or religious groups, covering all countries in the world.

People craves inclusion in these social phenomena to reduce their level of fear of the unknown, which is the underlying effect produced by the major linchpin of the satanic hack—self-preservation. However, by their sheer numbers and humanity's distorted concept of reality, the explosive growth of religious adherents only heightens the level confusion and conflict that already exist in our world. Needless to say, nowhere else is this phenomenon more

---

[9]https://adherents.com.cutestat.com

clearly seen than in the Christian religion. It just so happens that Christianity, with more than 2.4 billion[10] adherents, is the largest, and probably the most divided, religion in the world, with over 33,830 denominations.[11]

Christians are inclined to view their brand of Christianity through the broken lens of their hacked humanity and not through the reality of the life of the Christ they profess to serve. They worship and serve God through an identity based predominantly on a physical, not a spiritual reality—one mostly driven by their physical senses and intellect, and not by the born-again spirit of Jesus within them. While visiting a certain country, I met a pastor of a particular denomination who, during the course of our conversation, said to me very plainly: "If you could cut me up into a million little pieces, every piece will be labeled _____." The label was the initials of the denominational banner under which he serves. Needless to say, I was sadly disappointed, for the life of Jesus he professed to have received in place of his own at the time of his conversion was not the focus of the identity he so confidently dissected into bits.

Christians are inclined to view their brand of Christianity through the broken lens of their hacked humanity...

Whenever Christians choose to identify themselves by the image of their denomination or believing community, rather than the image of Jesus that God has recreated in their inner spirit-man,[12] they are prone to be judgmental of others who appear different than themselves. In a very subtle way, it is the expression of their defense mechanism in their effort to preserve their mistaken identity. This is

---

[10]Ibid.

[11]https://www.christianitytoday.com/ct/topics/d/denominations/

[12]See Romans 8:28, 29; Ephesians 3:14-19; Colossians 1:24-29.

exactly what people do who are totally racial in their outlook. Their sense of SELF feels vulnerable against the expression of the SELF identification of another. On a larger scale, Christian denominations tend to focus more on the issues they perceive that distinguish them from one another rather than on the eternal, spiritual reality[13] that unites them—the Spirit and Life of Jesus.

This phenomenon is driven by an identity corruption within Christianity that is an outgrowth of the satanic hack that facilitates self-preservation on a collective level. In this case, the denomination or organization seeks to preserve itself by assuming an identity that is independent of its authentic identity that it shares with all other Christians—Jesus Christ. In other words, denominations are quite willing to ignore the unity of Christ's spirit in ALL true believers and cling to an alternative false reality for self-preserving, denominational survival.

denominations are quite willing to ignore the unity of Christ's spirit in ALL true believers and cling to an alternative false reality for self-preserving, denominational survival.

How much is this attitude really different from that which precipitates racial tensions and conflicts in our world when the same damaged image of Adam[14] exists in all humanity? Institutional identity confusion also leads to the unhealthy scenario in which the denomination or institution will value and preserve its own life at the expense of the lives of the adherents who support it. Self-preservation and fear, individual or institutional, always lead to personal or

---

[13]Ephesians 4:4-6; John 17:20-23.
[14]Genesis 5:3 – *And Adam lived one hundred and thirty years, and begot [fathered] a son in his own likeness, after his image, and named him Seth*. Only Adam and Eve were **created** in the image of God before the Fall. However, after Adam fell from God's grace, all his descendants were **born** in his depraved likeness, after his fallen image.

organizational exploitation and/or abuse of others.

Humanity's identity corruption and all the social, religious and even political ills are unwelcome realities of our present world. Even with our best efforts to mitigate the threat they posed to our survival, the outlook for our success appears to be eluding us. Satan's hack of the human race has done such untold damage to our perception of reality and our ability to engage with the unseen, that without divine help, it will be totally impossible for us to save ourselves from existential misery and aggravating wretchedness. Humanity needs deliverance and it certainly cannot come from within what is already hacked and corrupt. Our only hope of rescue is from above.

O Lord, I know the way of man is not in himself; It is not in man who walks to direct his own steps. [24]O Lord, correct me, but with justice; not in Your anger, lest You bring me to nothing.

Jeremiah 10:23

10

The Hack and Human Restlessness

Having one's computer hacked causes great frustration because of the total loss of control over the machine and the important information it contains. As I mentioned at the beginning of this book, I had no way of deleting the racy images the hacker was posting on my wife's computer because he would only replace them with many, many more. The great losses and sheer annoyance in dealing with a hack computer network force companies and agencies to pay hefty ransoms to cyber criminals to retrieve stolen data or to regain some measure of control over their network.

In a very similar fashion, the devil's hack of humanity has disrupted the internal control of God's life in the human soul and has made the race vulnerable to demonic manipulation and heartless exploitation. In this penultimate chapter of The Hack of Humanity, we will explore how Satan's insidious incursion into the very psyche of humanity has precipitated a state of continuous restlessness that pushes the race to all types of extreme and excessive behaviors.[15] Although the average person may be quite reluctant to admit it, we do not have absolute control over the affairs of our lives as we often pretend to project. I illustrated this

---

[15]Ephesians 2:1-3; 4:18, 19.

in a few test questions in the introduction of this book. In this prevailing state of affairs, the words of the prophet Jeremiah ring true: *O Lord, I know the way of man is not in himself; it is not in man who walks to direct his own steps* (Jeremiah 10:23).

The apostle Paul, more than any other biblical figure, illustrated the reality of the human hack and the irritation it presents to a person in his exhausting pursuit of lasting peace and happiness. He spoke very candidly about his own lack of control and restlessness in his hopeless attempts to quiet his tormented soul.

> *[14]So the trouble is not with the law, for it is spiritual and good. The trouble is with me, for I am all too human, a slave to sin. [15]**I don't really understand myself**, for I want to do what is right, but I don't do it. Instead, I do what I hate. [16]But if I know that what I am doing is wrong, this shows that I agree that the law is good. [17]So I am not the one doing wrong; **it is sin living in me that does it.** [18]And I know that nothing good lives in me, that is, in my sinful nature. I want to do what is right, but I can't. [19]I want to do what is good, but I don't. I don't want to do what is wrong, but I do it anyway. [20]But if I do what I don't want to do, I am not really the one doing wrong; **it is sin living in me that does it**.*

> *[21]I have discovered this principle of life—that when I want to do what is right, I inevitably do what is wrong. [22]I love God's law with all my heart. [23]But **there is another power within me***

that is at war with my mind. This power makes me a slave to the sin that is still within me. <u>24Oh, what a miserable person I am</u>! <u>Who will free me from this life that is dominated by sin and death</u>?

Roman 7:14-23, NLT, emphasis mine

No doubt, Paul's dilemma reflects to some degree the human ignorance of "what lies beneath"[16] in every soul, actively working against our best intentions. Jesus was the only one in all the Scriptures who knew what that deceptive lurking element was, and the disciple John gave us a hint of this (John 2:24, 25). In the above passage, Paul refers to this dangerous, toxic element as "*sin living in me,*" and "*another power within me.*" These are clear references to the satanic hack of his humanity. Humanity's dilemma is its spirit-image separation from the continuous life and power of God, and its replacement by the rebellious, competitive virus of the human SELF—the oppositional spirit of Satan reigning as God in the human soul.

Sin and rebellion against God are ALWAYS the result of the self-resistant spirit of Satan working through the self-preserving reasoning of human intelligence. Their goal is ALWAYS to defend or to please the SELF before anyone or anything else. We sin whenever we attempt to please or defend the SELF. SELF-life demands survival at all cost because of its inherent fear of danger and death. Eternal life through spirit union with God does not. Self-preservation is the standing order of the SELF-life

SELF-life demands survival at all cost because of its inherent fear of danger and death.

---

[16]Words borrowed from 2000 movie by the same title, *"What Lies Beneath."*

virus in humanity and the driving force behind all natural human reason. Consequently, we fall short of our most noble intentions to please God because of our lack of faith in Him. Essentially, unbelief is the foundation of all sin and rebellion and represents an in-the-moment transference of sovereignty and power from God to the other god, SELF.[17] Truly, this is the "other power" Paul describes in the above scriptures as warring against his noblest thoughts, putting him in a place of servitude and utter wretchedness.

No doubt, we all have experienced the apostle's frustration in dealing with our own inability to control undesirable thoughts and behaviors. Many professed Christians are confronted daily with the dilemma of evil thoughts, sins, weaknesses, attitudes and addictions that they cannot seem to shake, even with their best efforts. Hidden behind the facade of their smiling faces and glowing public testimonies are the discouraging battles against the painful, crippling issues that have plagued their lives for years.

> *unbelief is the foundation of all sin and rebellion and represents an in the moment transference of sovereignty and power from God to the other god, SELF—really Satan.*

New Year resolutions, self-improvement plans and the like are dashed to pieces within the first few months of any given year. Healthy living plans—wholesome diet, gym attendance, exercise programs—and other positive initiatives soon dissipate when the pressures of life encroach, and motivation falls away. People soon find themselves back where they once were. Like the distraught apostle, the

---

[17]*Then He [Jesus] said to them all, "If anyone desires to come after Me, let him deny himself [the other god], and take up his cross daily, and follow Me* (Luke 9:23, brackets mine). The cross is for the daily crucifixion of the other god (SELF— Satan's undercover alias).

things they planned to do ended up not being done, and the very things they hated and were determined to avoid reared their ugly, repulsive heads again. Oh, what human wretchedness the hack of Satan has wrought!

The viral SELF-life deceives people into thinking that they have total control of their future and destiny, when in truth and in fact, they don't. They make what they believe to be iron-clad plans for their future—trusting in their savvy financial investments and their material accumulations—only to be cheated by unforeseen circumstances, including severe illness and "untimely" death. "Gone too soon" has become the standing label on the house of the dead. My father had great plans for my mother and himself after retirement, but he exited this life without touching a penny of his savings, pension or retirement benefits. I am pretty certain that he was not the only one of his kind. Many make plans for their lives, and rightly so, because of the unpredictability of the

> *"Gone too soon" has become the standing label on the house of the dead.*

future. However, they quite often forget or ignore the purpose of God as an overriding factor in all of their planning. The Bible tells us that *many are the plans in a person's heart, but it is the Lord's purpose that prevails* (Proverbs 19:21, NIV).

Because of humanity's disconnection from authentic reality—God and whatever He decrees—people make choices that they envision will bring them joy and peace, only to be appalled by the devastating, painful results they often yield. How often we hear of the horrific stories of women in very abusive relationships who initially thought their "knights in shining armor" would be the true love of their life. The opposite has been proven to be equally true—the beautiful woman who showed up looking, walking, talking and even singing like an angel turned out to be a dreadful, sad disappointment. Many people, young and old, often end up in places where they never thought they would have been—including tumultuous relationships, prison and painful addictions—because of making decisions they thought would have brought them wealth, fame, joy and life-changing happiness. The Bible makes this point very clear,

There is a way that seems right to a man, but its end is the way of death.

Proverbs 16:25

However, the most surreal outcome of the hack of humanity is that unknowingly people often plot their own misfortune and "untimely" demise. Painfully, most people are unaware that the words they speak are the life-giving expressions of the broken image of God in them. Words are NEVER empty. They are enormously powerful, and capable of altering a person's life situation for better or worse. Words matter. The Bible warns: *Death and life are in the power of the tongue, and those who love it will eat its fruits* (Proverbs 18:21). Those who choose to chatter indiscriminately put their lives and the lives of others at great risk without even realizing it. Moreover, because satanic hacking has predisposed humanity to a world of fear and negativity, the "prince of the power of the air"[18] uses our words against us. Here is how inspiration explains the powerful effects of the human tongue:

> *Words are NEVER empty. They are enormously powerful, and capable of altering a person's life situation for better or worse. Words matter.*

---

[18]*This is one of the aliases of the devil. Ephesians 2:1-3*

²Indeed, we all make many mistakes. For <u>if we could control our tongues, we would be perfect and could also control ourselves in every other way</u>. ³We can make a large horse go wherever we want by means of a small bit in its mouth. ⁴And a small rudder makes a huge ship turn wherever the pilot chooses to go, even though the winds are strong. ⁵In the same way, <u>the tongue is a small thing that makes grand speeches</u>. But <u>a tiny spark can set a great forest on fire</u>. ⁶And among all the parts of the body, <u>the tongue is a flame of fire</u>. <u>It is a whole world of wickedness</u>, <u>corrupting your entire body</u>. <u>It can set your whole life on fire</u>, for <u>it is set on fire by hell itself</u>. ⁷People can tame all kinds of animals, birds, reptiles, and fish, ⁸but <u>no one can tame the tongue</u>. <u>It is restless and evil, full of deadly poison</u>.

James 3:2-6, NLT, emphasis mine

This is quite an alarming passage! Most notable is the fact that though the tongue is among the smallest members of our body, it is quite an unruly instrument of destruction. According to our text, this little muscular organ is capable not only of corrupting the whole person, but also of setting his entire life ablaze with all kinds of trouble. Most people are unaware of the inseparable connection between their tongue and the depraved spirit image of their Creator within them. They are of the opinion that their words are just the product of their intelligence, and do not give due diligence to the attitudes and moods—yeah, the corrupted spirit—that drive them. However, the devil understands this powerful linkage and uses it to fuel confusion and conflict, incite wars and wanton human mayhem and devastation. It is for this very reason the above scripture says that the tongue is set ablaze by hell to spread the fires of destruction in our lives.

When the invisible God created this world, He spoke everything into existence.[19] What God said mattered. His words were not hollow, and what resulted was an immaculate creation generated by His perfect Spirit. Moreover, when the Designer breathed His own spirit image into humanity, that image gave humankind the ability to shape its environment and the course of human history by the perfect, disciplined use of the tongue. However, the moment the first family corrupted itself through spiritual alienation from God, the speech patterns of the race were permanently tainted, becoming negative, poisonous and quite deadly.[20]

What God said mattered. His words were not hollow, and what resulted was an immaculate creation generated by His perfect Spirit.

I can tell of many true-life stories of how words have changed the lives of people I have encountered in all my travels. How often have parents spoken horrible, negative words over their children in order to "scare them stiff" into better behavior only to be devastated by the deadly outcome of the words from their own lips. More recently, time seemed to have stood still when the gut-wrenching news of the "untimely" passing of basketball legend, Kobe Bryant, hit the airwaves. I later discovered via a video interview by one of his very close friends, Tracy McGrady,

---

[19]In Genesis 1, the words *"and God said"* occur at least 9 times. SEE also Psalm 33:6-9 and Hebrews 11:3.
[20]Review the five symptoms of satanic hacking in Chapter 7. SEE also James 3:6-9.

that the youthful Kobe spoke repeatedly of his desire for an early exit off this world's stage as an "immortalized" legend.[21] How unbelievably surreal that the seeds of these words planted many years ago, and probably forgotten by Kobe himself, germinated to bear this extremely bitter fruit of hurtful loss and overwhelming brokenness. His precious family, the families of the other crash victims, and the family of hurting, dazed fans were left quite devastated, while they clinged to every precious memory of him!

Our words do matter, and the evil one knows that quite well. He intentionally makes use of this knowledge to keep humanity in bondage and utter confusion. Satan also knows that left to itself, humanity is incapable of controlling it fire-starting, death-dealing tongue. Just as a rider uses a bridle and a bit in a horse's mouth to control the body and movement of the powerful creature, so the devil employs the fearful, negative self-preserving virus in the human soul to put pressure on the tongue to control the course of human existence. It is the corruption of this soul virus that drives the uncontrollable speech of the tongue, which, in turn, brings injury, pain and disaster to the life. Jesus once spoke to this truth when He chided the Pharisees about their evil disposition and conduct.

> *Our words matter, and the evil one knows that quite well.*

> [34]*Brood of vipers! How can you, being evil, speak good things?* ***For out of the abundance of the heart the mouth speaks.*** [35]*A good man out of the good treasure of his heart [righteous soul]*

---

[21]Tracy McGrady's interview with ESPN's Rachel Nichols. https://www.huffpost.com/entry/kobe-bryant-i-want-to-die-young_n_5e300b89c5b68f86c8cdac5f.

*brings forth good things, and an evil man out
of the evil treasure [of his corrupt soul] brings
forth evil things. [36]But I say to you that for every
idle word men [people] may speak, they will
give account of it in the day of judgment. [37]For
<u>by your words you will be justified, and by your
words you will be condemned</u>."*

Matthew 12:34-37, brackets and emphasis mine

Therefore, it is not surprising that the Bible says that
*if we could control our tongues, we would be perfect and
could also control ourselves in every other way* (James 3:2,
NLT). However, Jesus tells us that the control mechanism
for our fire-starting tongue is a well-cultivated heart—really
a spirit-directed soul, for our tongue cannot speak from
anywhere else. Consequently, the Bible counsels us, *"Guard
your heart above all else, for it determines the course of
your life"* (Proverbs 4:23, NLT), via the portal of our mouth.[22]
It is also of paramount importance for us to remember that
just as the tongue has power to produce devastation and
death in one's life, it also possesses the authority to cancel
ill-spoken words and generate the blessings of life, health,
peace and joy through words fitly spoken.

Stressful Human Living

The most crippling display of humanity's quest to
be like God,[23] to think and act independently of Him—the

---

[22] *. . . For out of the abundance of the heart the mouth speaks* (Matthew 12:34).
[23]Satan's words to Eve: *For God knows that in the day you eat of it your eyes will be
opened, and <u>you will be like God</u>, knowing good and evil* – Genesis 3:5.

core element of the satanic hack—is the increasing burden of stress it places upon the race. The moment Adam and Eve separated themselves from God and eternal life, they were faced with the very stressful worry of preserving their lives by their human efforts. They wanted to be like God but were oblivious to the taxing liabilities that such a decision would imposed upon them and their descendants. Life became quite uncertain and troublesome. The very creation, once amenable to their rule, competed with them for mere survival, for everything groaned under the curse of death because of human transgression. To this very day, humanity continues to inflict severe abuses upon the environment for its own selfish ends.

However, we were never designed by our Creator to operate successfully independent of Him. Human reason alone is totally inadequate to deal with all the uncertainties and burdens that sin and the hack have levied upon the race. Stress and mental anguish have become a normal part of human life only because of the hacking effect of self-preservation. Moreover, the human brain, divinely ordered to be the servant of God's righteous spirit-image in humanity, became severely overtaxed and functionally compromised by ceaseless worry and stress. The overall result of all this is the chaotic breakdown of mental, emotional and bodily functions.

Human reason alone is totally inadequate to deal with all the uncertainties and burdens that sin and the hack have levied upon the race.

What is Stress Really?

According to Dr. William C. Shiel Jr, "in a medical or

biological context stress is a physical, mental, or emotional factor that causes bodily or mental tension. Stresses can be external (from the environment, psychological, or social situations) or internal (illness, or from a medical procedure)."[24] The Merriam-Webster Dictionary[25] states that stress is (a) a physical, chemical, or emotional factor that causes bodily or mental tension and may be a factor in disease causation; and (b) a state of bodily or mental tension resulting from factors that tend to alter an existent equilibrium. In all these definitions, it is very clear to observe that stress has an effect on the total well-being of a person.

However, in the context of this book, stress is really the negative reactions of our vital life forces resulting from the failure of our self-preserving efforts to be like God over all our ill-perceived situations. This unspoken generational lie[26] that drives people to believe that they have the ability to solve all their problems is the sole perpetrator of human stress and restlessness. Even if humanity was able to solve ALL of its perceived problems, including total cancellation of death, our world will still be a very stressful, unmanageable place because of Satan's SELF-life virus in the human soul. SELF-life, with its self-centered disposition, is a stress producer in any "perfect" environment, if such could ever exist in any progressive, sophisticated world. The unwelcome truth is, God ALONE is Sovereign. He is the ONLY Self-existent One in the universe with life that is unborrowed and underived.

> *stress is really the negative reactions of our vital life forces resulting from the failure of our self-preserving efforts to be like God...*

---

[24]William C. Shiel Jr., MD, FACP, FACR, *Medical Definition of Stress*, at https://www.medicinenet.com/script/main/art.asp?articlekey=20104.
[25]https://www.merriam-webster.com/dictionary/stress.
[26]Satan's words to Eve. Genesis 3:4, 5 – *"... you will be like God..."*

Quality of Life

Stress is a function of the mind that adversely affects the brain. The mind is the expression of the human spirit—the marred image of God in humanity. It is very important to remember that the brain is physical matter, and that at creation it was Divine thought—immaterial Spirit—that created all physical matter. This Divine Mind of the immaterial God was shared by His human creation via His spirit-image in humanity, to govern the activities of the physical brain and body. The brain was not designed to hold sway over the mind, but to facilitate the thoughts and expressions of the mind. Communication pathologist and cognitive neuroscientist, Dr. Caroline Leaf, rightly affirms that "our mind is designed to control the body, of which the brain is a part, not the other way around. Matter does not control us; we control matter through our thinking and choosing."[27] Consequently, the brain is what the mind does, not the mind being what the brain does.[28] Apart from the spirit-mind the brain is dead.[29]

Matter does not control us; we control matter through our thinking and choosing.

Without this clear understanding of the relationship between the spirit-mind and the brain, it would be impossible for anyone to see how Satan's hack against God's spirit-image in humanity has an ongoing impact on the quality of life on this planet. It is the powerful thoughts of the mind that drive the physical activities of the brain to govern all the functions in, and actions of, the body. The impact of our thoughts on our brain is quite phenomenal. Neuroscience

---

[27]Caroline Leaf, *Switch on Your Brain* (Grand Rapid: Baker Books, 2013), 33.
[28]Ibid, 31-32.
[29]James 2:26 – *...the body without the spirit is dead...*

reveals that our brain is neuroplastic. This means that our brain is malleable and adaptable, capable of changing its structure and expression through the power of the mind. Dr. Leaf[30] states that as we think, we change physical nature of our brain by wiring thought patterns, positive or toxic, into or out of it. Moreover, these thoughts, through genetic expressions and chemical reactions, translate into real, mental real estate and physical activity in our brain and our body.

...the brain is what the mind does, not the mind being what the brain does.

Why is all this so relevant to our conversation on demonic hacking and the permanent stress factors associated with human restlessness? Because Satan makes use of this neuro-biological relationship to confuse and corrupt the neurological functions of the brain. Such disruption causes toxic chemical reactions that poison and undermine the biological functions of the body, making it vulnerable to sickness and disease. This is exactly what happens when the mind and body become the victims of prolonged, overbearing stress. Caroline Leaf says that "an undisciplined mind is filled with a continuous stream of worries, fears and distorted perceptions that trigger degenerative processes in the mind and body."[31] These mental, emotional and physical stress factors have an undeniably huge adverse impact on the quality of human life.

Stress and Human Illness

Through a variety of well-documented sources, Dr.

---

[30]Ibid, 20, 32.
[31]Ibid, 76.

Leaf corroborated evidence that 75 to 98 percent of mental and physical illness comes from stress associated with one's thought life.[32] This is quite staggering! Moreover, when we combine this statistic with the negative side effects from all the man-made chemicals infused into the human body to deal with symptomatic illness and disease resulting from stressful thinking, we could see quite easily the unmanageable human crises we have on our hands. Mental, emotional and physical illnesses continue to climb, and drug companies strengthen their grip on the masses with a proliferation of new drugs and fear-inducing advertising in the marketplace.

Here is the breakdown of the sad truth behind all of this. Satan's hack of humanity led to spiritual and physical separation from the eternal life of God and elevated his viral seed of the human SELF to rule over the soul. This disconnection and functional distortion gave rise to the overpowering effect of the hacking force of self-preservation and all the fears precipitated by it. It is the prevailing fear factor of humanity that drives all the negative, stressful thinking of people in their attempt to avert human discomforts, pain and death.

In 2005, the National Science Foundation published an article showing that the average person has between 12,000 and 60,000 thoughts per day, of which 80% are negative, and 95% are exactly the same as the day before. These statistics are quite frightening, to say the least, and only helps to validate the reality of Satan's hacking of the human race. Humanity is prone to negativity because of all the fears and stresses associated with the pervasive influence of self-preservation. This very unwholesome,

---

[32]Ibid, 37-38.

negative environment produces high levels of chemical toxicity in the human brain and body that contribute to all types of mental, emotional and physical ailments. Sadly, these deadly results only help to elevate fear and anxiety in people, and set the stage for cyclical stress, sickness, disease and untimely death.

Needless to say, the hack of humanity is very real, and unknowingly, the masses march along to the deadly beat of the debilitating virus in the human soul. However, there is hope for all humanity if we could turn the race's attention to its Creator and Designer for deliverance, healing, recovery and total redemption. The upcoming final chapter will open a window into God's answer to Satan's plot against humanity and how we all benefit from it. However, the full treatment of that response will be dealt with in my next volume, *The ReGened Life, Humanity's Hope After the Hack.*

[12]Salvation is found in no one else, for there is no other name under heaven given to mankind by which we must be saved.

Acts 4:12, NIV

11

The Only Way Out

We have spent the last ten chapters of this book exploring how Satan hacked humanity, the damage it has done to the image of God in the race, and the ongoing adverse effects that impairment has on human life and on our world. In this chapter, we will open the door into the only positive and productive alternative available to all the generations of fallen Adam. The sad reality is that with all its intelligence and investigations humanity has not been able to, and cannot, save itself from itself and the deceitful destruction of its own imaginations. A hacked computer cannot change its default setting or operating system without the direct input of its owner. In the very same manner, hacked humanity cannot repair or change its damaged soul and false perception of reality without the direct intervention of its original Designer—God.

Although humanity has produced many bright and hopeful lights who momentarily lift the dismal outlook of mankind's future, these shooting stars quickly faded away, only to be replaced by others as the cycles of disappointment rumbled on. Henry Francis Lyte rightly captures this disillusionment in the second verse of his well-loved hymn,

"Abide with Me."[33] He wrote:

Swift to its close ebbs out life's little day
Earth's joys grow dim, its glories pass away
Change and decay in all around I see
O Thou who changest not, abide with me

In this remarkable hymn, the author was comparing the fleeting nature of humanity and all its accomplishments with the only unchanging Reality that he knew, and was appealing for His abiding presence in the ebb and flow of his very short life.

The Bible is very clear in its assessment of humanity's ability to save itself from the dilemma of satanic hacking. In the book of Acts, we read the very powerful statement: *Neither is there salvation in any other: for there is none other name under heaven given among men, whereby we must be saved* (Acts 4:12, KJV). That name is Jesus, God's Savior and Gift to the human race. He is the only hope for humanity's deliverance from the dominion of the evil one.

Creator in the Hacking Zone

[16]For God so loved the world that He gave His only begotten Son, that whoever believes in Him should not perish but have everlasting life. [17]For God did not send His Son into the world to condemn the world, but that the world through Him might be saved.

John 3:16, 17

---

[33]Hymn by Scottish writer, Henry Francis Lyte, 1847.

The above scripture assures us that the God who created the world and humanity has not abandoned the planet to the whim and wickedness of the vengeful hacker. Although Adam and Eve made the fatal choice to break their spirit-union with the Creator and aligned themselves and their generations with the evil one, God did not give up on the special object of His love. He did not even wait for them to make the first move for reconciliation and reunification. He did. It was God Who went in search of the guilty, fallen pair that was attempting to "hide"[34] from His presence. God always makes the first move in regard to the redemption of the fallen race. This gracious act ignites every human desire for Him.

It is also very important to recognize that God's posture toward humanity is not one of condemnation, but one of redeeming love, reconciliation and redemption. *God did not send His Son into the world to condemn the world, but that the world through Him might be saved* (John 3:17). As I stated previously, God entered the hacking zone of our world in the person of His Son, Jesus Christ, to reconcile the world to Himself. Let's read this powerful scripture again: *...God was reconciling the world to himself in Christ, <u>not counting people's sins against them</u>. And he has committed to us the message of reconciliation* (2 Corinthians 5:19, NIV, emphasis mine). The Father was intimately present in Jesus throughout His brief earthly life. It was the Savior Himself

> God always makes the first move in regard to the redemption of the fallen race. This gracious act ignites every human desire for Him.

---

[34]A reference to Adam's distorted view of reality; for he supposed that he was able to hide from the omniscient, omnipresent One who created Him. What a fallacious idea!

who said. *"...He who has seen Me has seen the Father... the Father who dwells in Me does the works. Believe Me that I am in the Father and the Father in Me..."* (John 14:9-11).

The gospel of John gives us another informative glimpse of this mysterious union of the Creator, and our Father, and the Word,[35] Jesus Christ. In this unique picture, we see God, expressing Himself through the Son, in His rescue mission of humanity and His creation.

> *In the beginning was the Word, and the Word was with God, and the Word was God. [2]He [the Word] was in the beginning with God. [3]All things were made through Him, and without Him nothing was made that was made... [14]And the Word became flesh and dwelt among us, and we beheld His glory, the glory as of the only begotten of the Father, full of grace and truth.*
>
> John 1:1-3, 14

Over and over again, the Scriptures express the truth that Jesus was the exact representation of God, the Father in our hacked world. In Hebrews 1:3 we see Him as the brightness of God's glory and the express image of His person. In 2 Corinthians 4:4, the apostle Paul referenced the glory of Christ as the image of God.

Consequently, in Christ, God came to our world to take care of humanity's sin problem and to restore the race to its rightful place in relation to Himself. Humanity originated in God and simply cannot exist holistically without unbroken union with Him. It is this holistic, consuming love of God

---

[35] The Word is a theological reference to the Son, Jesus Christ. SEE John 1:14

THE ONLY WAY OUT

that moved the Creator to be identified with the plight of humanity and give Himself, through the Godman, Jesus Christ, for the life of the world. This is so astounding for the human mind to grasp. As a direct result, sinners

> *Humanity originated in God and simply cannot exist holistically without unbroken union with Him.*

continue to run away from God, and among those who have chosen to follow Christ, God is still held in suspicion. Many equate God's love with sinlessness and cannot conceive of God loving them in spite of their broken humanity. For this very reason, God had to manifest Himself in human flesh so that we could experience the tangibility of His redeeming love and grace.

The Mission of the Savior

[14]Since the children have flesh and blood, he too shared in their humanity so that by his death he might break the power of him who holds the power of death—that is, the devil— [15]and free those who all their lives were held in slavery by their fear of death.

Hebrews 2:14, 15, NIV

The incarnation of God in the person of Jesus Christ has a specific goal in mind—that is, total destruction of the hacker and his power of death enslavement over humanity. Christ entered our hacking zone to eradicate completely all the evil works of Satan and to liberate all who would receive His offer for their ransom and redemption. The Bible states that *the Son of God appeared for this purpose, to destroy the works of the devil* (1 John 3:8, NASB). God's redemptive purpose is to cancel the destructive legacy Adam gave to humanity, and replace it with the incorruptible legacy of Jesus Christ, Adam's replacement and Father of a new, born-again race. The Scriptures record this irrevocable truth,

> *[12]Therefore, just as sin entered the world through <u>one man</u>, and death through sin, and in this way death came to all people, because all sinned... [17]For if, by the trespass of the one man [Adam], **death reigned** through that one man, how much more will <u>those who receive</u> God's abundant provision of grace and of <u>the gift of righteousness</u> **reign in life** through the <u>one man, Jesus Christ</u>... [19]For just as through the **disobedience** of the one man the many were made sinners, so also through the obedience of <u>the one</u> man <u>the many</u> will be made **righteous**. [20]God's law was given so that all people could see how sinful they were. But as people sinned more and more, God's wonderful grace became more abundant.*

> Romans 5:12, 17, 19, NIV, emphasis mine

These verses of scripture encapsulate the depth and marvel of God's redemptive love for the fallen human race. The destructive scourge brought by satanic hacking is completely swallowed up by the abundant gift of God's redeeming grace through the one Godman, Jesus Christ. God made it impossible for the plague of sin to overwhelm the scope and power of His love for humanity; for *wherever sin abounded, God's grace abounded much more* (Romans 5:20).

It is of utmost importance to see in the above scriptures how God took care of the viral transmission of Adam's sinful legacy, by applying the cancelling effect of the viral transmission of the righteous legacy of our Savior, Jesus Christ. Notice, on the one hand, **the one (Adam)**, for **the many fallen humanity,** brought the curse of sin, bondage and death. On the other hand, **the many**, by **the one (Jesus Christ),** receive the free gift of grace, righteousness, freedom and eternal life. Death reigned—like a king—from **the one** to **the many**; but eternal Life reigned—like it's King—over **the many** by **the one**, Jesus Christ. *Oh, the depth of the riches both of the wisdom and knowledge of God! How unsearchable are His judgments and His ways past finding out* (Romans 11:33)!

This magnanimous move of God to secure our eternal salvation through the free Gift of Jesus Christ is so astounding that it seems hard for many people to believe. Humanity's self-centeredness and self-effort from satanic hacking make this an impassable barrier even for many professed followers of Jesus. They just cannot believe that they could do absolutely nothing to save themselves. Pride and self-worth often inhibit them from simply trusting God and accepting His free gift of righteousness and eternal life. Many spend their few days on the planet still striving at the impossible task of cleaning up their Adamic existence to get it ready for heaven, when God has already given them the incorruptible seed of Christ's perfect life in their spirit already fitted for heaven. The whole purpose of the next book[36] to follow this one is to bring believers into the reality of the seed of Jesus's life in the here and now. Righteousness has never been something for believers to achieve; it has

---

[36]*The ReGened Life, Humanity Hope After the Hack* is a current work in progress.

always been God's free gift for every believer to receive and keep on receiving.

The mission of Jesus to destroy the hacking works of the devil and guarantee his final extinction is a done deal. When, in His last, dying breath, our Savior cried out, "It is finished," He was not only announcing the end of Satan's kingdom and its terrestrial hacking activity; He was guaranteeing

> *Righteous has never been something for believers to achieve; it has always been God's free gift for every believer to receive and keep on receiving.*

a brand new beginning and future to all who would receive His sacrifice for all their sins. The completion of Christ's redemptive mission is God's assurance for humanity's eternal salvation. He has already set the table and has invited all to partake. Will you accept His invitation?

Ready for Change

> *Therefore, if anyone is in Christ, he is a new creation; old things have passed away; behold, all things have become new.*
>
> 2 Corinthians 5:17-20

The door of salvation from the hack of humanity has been left ajar for everyone and anyone, without qualification, to enter it. In the parable of The Good Shepherd, Christ calls Himself the door. He says, *"I am the door. If anyone enters by Me, he will be saved, and will go in and out and find pasture"* (John 10:7). Through the Savior, Jesus Christ, God is offering every human being the incomparable opportunity to start life over and really enjoy doing it. Our main text for this section tells us that if anyone receives life in Jesus Christ, that person becomes a completely new creation of God. From God's standpoint, everything about his old life beyond his physical appearance, is utterly erased, and he stands as a brand-new creature before his Redeemer. This divine act of the Creator is not contingent upon human opinions, reasons or feelings. It is the sovereign work of God's love and grace alone. As a matter of fact, the Bible clearly states:

> *But as many as received Him [Jesus], to them He [God] gave the right to become children of God, to those who believe in His [Jesus] name:* **[13]who were born**, *not of blood, nor of the will of the flesh, nor of the will of man, but* **of God**.

John 1:12, 13

This text speaks of the many, but the purposeful removal of the letter "m" will yield the word "any," which opens the door of reception to anyone. Whoever receives Jesus Christ—that is, His sacrificial death and resurrected life in place of his life of sin and impending damnation—and believe in His name, is given the divine right by God Himself to become His child. This exclusive right cannot be taken away or annulled by anyone or any earthly authority. Not only that! Please do not miss the next part of this very important scripture. It says that a miraculous birth takes place in the spirit realm whenever a person makes that life-changing decision to receive Jesus Christ as his Savior and Lord. That person is born again, but this time around it is not a natural flesh and blood experience. This life is born of God! Many professed believers miss or misunderstand this reality and continue to define themselves and their situations from the natural point of view. Consequently, they come to the born-again experience with a behavior modification orientation. Nothing like this is further from the truth.

There is absolutely nothing natural about being born of God, and when correctly

There is absolutely nothing natural about being born of God

understood and appropriated, it equips and empowers the believer to rebuff successfully the schemes and devices of the evil hacker. Being born of God and born of man are two incompatible and irreconcilable experiences that must be clearly understood and that would take more than this chapter to explain. Briefly speaking, however, what is born of man is mere human, but what is born of God is immaculately divine. What is born of man is flesh—or moves only by human reason, but what is born of God is spirit—or directed only by His spirit image within. Moreover, what is born of man is overcome by this hacked world systems, but *what is born of God has already overcome the world* (1 John 5:4). In short, whoever receives Christ as Savior and Lord is ReGened[37] in the life of God.

ReGened RSVP

Come to Me, all you who labor and are heavy laden, and I will give you rest. [29]Take My yoke upon you and learn from Me, for I am gentle and lowly in heart, and you will find rest for your souls. [30]For My yoke is easy, and My burden is light.

Matthew 11:28-30

---

[37]ReGened is my usage for the experience of a person being regenerated in God's image again.

I believe it is only fitting to end this book with the invitation of Jesus, God's ultimate answer for Satan's hack of humanity. He entered the devil's domain, soundly defeated him and established an impregnable platform to ReGene Adam's fallen race through His own incorruptible Life. What a wonderful Savior is Jesus our Lord! His invitation is quite simple but profoundly satisfying if accepted. Everyone still needs Him, even if the effects of Satan's hacking clouds the understanding of this need. No one can negotiate life successful in this crooked, failing world without the wisdom and guidance of Jesus's life on the inside. We do not have to look very far to see how our present world is crumbling all around us, while people struggle hopelessly, trying to make sense of everyday living.

If you are one of those people and life seems unfair to you, weighing you down with crushing cares and burdens, there's still hope for you. If you are fearful because of all the uncertainties in our troubled world, feeling stressed, distraught and depressed over your life's situations, please don't give up now. Jesus can give you the peace and rest you so desperately need if you will only turn to Him. He is able to give you a brand, new start. You do not have to remain a victim of satanic hacking, tormented by toxic thoughts that threaten your health. You can find true peace and freedom in Jesus. Precious reader, your Savior says to you right now, *"Come to Me... and find rest for your soul."*

Would you RSVP to this invitation today? Here is a simple prayer to help you do so.

> *"Dear Jesus, thank You for loving me in spite of myself. Thank You for dying for my sins and*

*offering me eternal life. I confess all my sins to
You, and I receive You as my Savior and Lord
right now. Please come into my life and make me
a new person from this day forward. I believe in
You and thank You for saving me, according to
Your word, amen."*

The moment you utter this prayer in sincerity, a
divine miracle occurs within you. Through the ministry of
His Spirit, God plants the incorruptible seed of Christ's
victorious, resurrected life in the inner man of your spirit
and you are born again of God Himself. This is an act of
faith on your part and will be the greatest decision of your
life. You may not have any instantaneous physical evidence
of God's acceptance or endorsement of your request; but
be assured that the God of your salvation ALWAYS answers
this prayer.

If, indeed, you said the above prayer, you are now a
bonafide child of God, and your heavenly Father has given
you every right to say so (John 1:12). Moreover, if you took
this significant step before, but still find yourself being
buffeted by the schemes of the evil hacker, my follow up
book will show you how to live triumphantly through the
incorruptible seed of Jesus' life within you.

Indeed, God has given us the only way out of the
debacle of satanic hacking. He has already guaranteed
our deliverance and salvation in Jesus Christ. The blessed
privilege is ours to lay hold of this free Gift (Jesus) of
grace, righteousness and abundant life and appropriate
the benefits of His amazing, transforming legacy right here
and now. Let's take the next critical step. Enter confidently
into the awesome experience of ReGened Life, our only

hope after the hack of humanity. My next volume[38] will show you how.

---

[38]*The ReGened Life, Humanity's Hope After the Hack.*

Don't Miss These Other Life-changing Resources

by Dr. Ruthven J. Roy

The Samson Xfile

The Samson Xfile is the intriguing review of the most misunderstood faith-hero in the Bible—Samson. Christian tradition has perpetuated a negative view of this God-warrior; but the mysterious Xfile (Judges 14:4) of God's providence paints an amazingly very different picture. See your life reflected in God's dealing with Samson.

ISBN: 978-0-9717853-2-8 (Paperback)

The Explosive Power of Network Discipling

"Every Christian is called to be a disciple of Jesus; and every disciple is called to be a fisher, not just a member!" In this volume Dr. Roy clearly explains Christ's master plan for growing His kingdom. Christ calls everyone to discipleship, not membership.

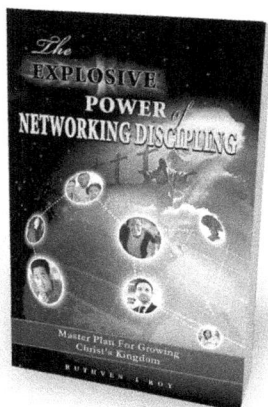

ISBN: 978-0-9717853-4-2

Imitating God

Imitating God is not only possible, but it is also guaranteed. This book will make available to you the key to your true identity, and will show you, in very simple steps, how to unleash the power of God's life from within you. Get ready to enter into the **God-zone**.

ISBN: 978-0-9717853-3-5

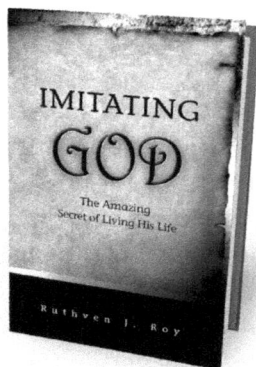

Study Guide: Imitating God

Do not forget this companion Study Guide to go along with this magnificent text. It would greatly enhance your understanding of all the vital issues that pertain to your spiritual identity and living victoriously. Moreover, this Study Guide will provide you with an exciting, hands-on way to share this good news with others.

ISBN: 978-0-9717853-6-6

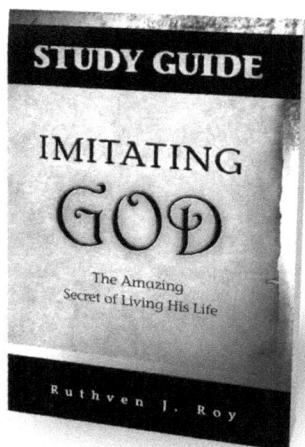

Unshakeable Kingdom

In the church, yet outside of God's kingdom! What a tragedy! Learn how to avoid the "Nicodemus Syndrome," the common sickness of modern Christianity! Understand true kingdom fitness and why religion is simply not enough. *The kingdom of heaven is NOW; not later! Later is TOO late!* This volume will change your focus and your life in a way that only a miracle from God can. *Seize the moment, and make the decision to enter God's Unshakeable Kingdom now!*

ISBN: 978-0-9717853-3-5

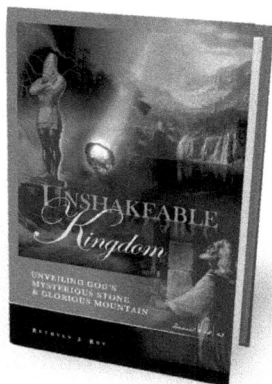

Position Yourself for Success

God knew and wrote our success story long before our arrival on this planet. True success depends on how we position ourselves in relation to God's purpose for our existence in this world. This book will help you to discover and pursue it!

ISBN: 978-0-9717853-8-0

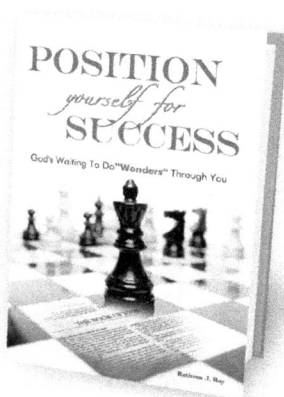

Born-Again Life

Born-again life is not an upgrade or a transformation of our life in Adam, but a total replacement of it. This life, though expressed through our physical humanity, has not a thread of humanity in it. It is absolutely incorruptible and totally divine, because it originated directly from the incorruptible God. If your born-again experience is everything else but exciting, restful, victorious and totally satisfying, then this book is guaranteed to be an abundant, life-transforming blessing to you.

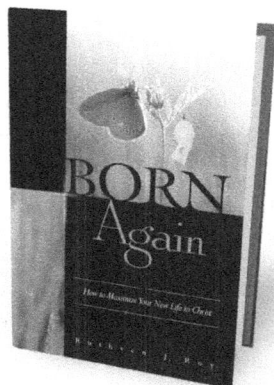

ISBN: 978-0-9717853-9-7

Available online or at your local Christian bookstore

For more information, visit www.roybooks.com,
or write to royjrbooks@gmail.com

Contact Information

Dr. Ruthven J. Roy

NETWORK DISCIPLING MINISTRIES
P.O. Box 33
Berrien Springs, MI 49103

Tel: (301) 514-2383
Email: ruthvenroy@gmail.com

RUTHVEN ROY is a discipleship and spiritual counseling consultant; and founder of Network Discipling Ministries. He and his wife Lyris live in Michigan, USA.

www.ingramcontent.com/pod-product-compliance
Lightning Source LLC
Chambersburg PA
CBHW071434090426
42737CB00011B/1660